United States
Department of
Agriculture

Forest Service

Southern
Research Station

General Technical
Report SRS–148

Louisiana's Palustris Experimental Forest: 75 Years of Research that Transformed the South

James P. Barnett, James D. Haywood, and Henry A. Pearson

Authors:

James P. Barnett, retired Chief Silviculturist, Emeritus Scientist, and **James D. Haywood**, Supervisory Research Forester, U.S. Department of Agriculture, Forest Service, Southern Research Station, Pineville, LA 71360; **Henry A. Pearson** worked most of his career as Project Leader and Chief Range Scientist, and is now Emeritus Scientist, U.S. Department of Agriculture, Forest Service, Southern Research Station, and retired from the USDA Agricultural Research Service.

Cover

The J.K. Johnson Tract of the Palustris Experimental Forest is located near Elmer, LA. Photograph was taken by Donald P. Feduccia for Thomas E. Campbell in the late 1970s.

Photo credits

Unless otherwise noted, the photographs are from collections of the U.S. Department of Agriculture, Forest Service, the Louisiana Forestry Commission (now Louisiana Department of Agriculture and Forestry), and the Louisiana Forestry Association. The organizations have extensive photographic collections, and many of the early photographs were interchanged among agencies. While working for these organizations, professional photographers Elemore Morgan and Tommy Kohara took many of the photographs.

Disclaimer

The use of trade or firm names in this publication is for reader information and does not imply endorsement by the U.S. Department of Agriculture of any product or service. Pesticide Precautionary Statement This publication reports research involving pesticides. It does not contain recommendations for their use, nor does it imply that the uses discussed here have been registered. All uses of pesticides must be registered by appropriate State and Federal agencies before they can be recommended.

Caution

Pesticides can be injurious to humans, domestic animals, desirable plants, and fish or other wildlife—if they are not handled or applied properly. Use all pesticides selectively and carefully. Follow recommended practices for disposal of surplus pesticides and pesticide containers.

November 2011

Southern Research Station
200 W. T. Weaver Blvd.
Asheville, NC 28804

Louisiana's Palustris Experimental Forest:
75 Years of Research that Transformed the South

James P. Barnett, James D. Haywood, and Henry A. Pearson

Abstract—The Palustris Experimental Forest, located on Kisatchie National Forest, has been in existence for 75 years. Research at Palustris has focused on southern pine reforestation technology, including seed production, bareroot nursery production, direct seeding, and planting container seedlings. After establishing pine plantations, researchers developed stand management guidelines for thinning, fertilizing, use of fire, stocking levels, and modeling of growth projections. Researchers elucidated knowledge of soil influences and plant competition, factors key to optimizing and maintaining plantation stand productivity. Researchers also emphasized range management that established guidelines for livestock utilization on forest ranges across the South. Today's forest industry across the South maximizes productivity with the management practices developed by researchers on the Palustris Experimental Forest.

Keywords: Agroforestry, history of southern forestry, pine plantation management, reforestation of southern pines, seed and seedling physiology

Contents

Introduction

In the late 1800s, forests in the United States were harvested with little regard for conserving or reforesting them. The combined threats of logging, wildfire, land clearing, and wildlife depletion called into question the supposed inexhaustibility of the Nation's forests.

As a result of this conservation impetus, U.S. Department of Agriculture, the Forest Service, was established in 1905. The chief of the newly created Forest Service, Gifford Pinchot, helped persuade U.S. President Theodore Roosevelt to develop and promote conservation as the "wise use" of natural resources (MacCleery 2002). Under the "wise use" view, resources were to be managed to protect the basic productivity of the land and its ability to serve future generations.

Supporting the "wise use" philosophy, the Forest Service in 1915 created a research branch for scientific and technical investigations. Soon after, the U.S. Congress expanded forestry research and authorized regional forestry research stations. In 1921, the Southern Forest Experiment Station was established with headquarters in New Orleans, LA, and the Appalachian Forest Experiment Station in Asheville, NC. The Southern Forest Experiment Station had research responsibility primarily for pine forests in the Coastal Plain region and the Appalachian Station for mountain hardwood forests of the Southeast.

Experimental forests have their genesis in the Great Depression (circa 1930s), when U.S. President Franklin D. Roosevelt's New Deal programs brought an influx of money and manpower to expanding conservation programs. With help from work crews in the Civilian Conservation Corps (CCC) and the Works Progress Administration (WPA), forest researchers began in earnest to create experimental forests across the Nation.

Most of these forests had a particular focus shaped by conservation needs of their particular region. Some of these forests were closed after meeting their immediate objectives, but others still serve ever changing research needs.

In 1935, the Palustris Experimental Forest was established in central Louisiana as a site for a program of evaluating outplanting trials of pine seedlings grown in nursery experimental studies. The program's goal was to provide scientific technology for reforesting millions of acres of denuded forest land throughout the South. The research initiative was successful, eventually forming the foundation for a published set of guidelines for southern pine reforestation, "Planting the Southern Pines" by Phillip C. Wakeley (1954).

The Palustris Experimental Forest expanded in 1950 following the 1946 establishment of the Alexandria Research Center in Pineville, LA. The purpose of the expansion was to provide technology that might minimize the adverse effects of cattle and hogs that ranged freely on denuded forest land and limited success of reforestation programs.

The Palustris Experimental Forest has met many other significant research needs. Today, it is a testing site for a wide array of interdisciplinary research programs. Over its 75-year history, research on the Palustris Experimental Forest changed how forestry is practiced across the South and produced programs that have positively affected the economic value of southern forests.

The major influences of pine forest research programs conducted on the Palustris Experimental Forest and their impact on expanding the southern economy is the focus of this recorded history.

The Need for Research

The original southern pine forests were awesome in their vastness. Interrupted by occasional bottomland swamps, pine forests stretched throughout the Coastal Plain from Virginia to the Texas plains in what the early settlers must have considered an endless expanse—a distance of nearly 1,500 miles. The longleaf pine forests were estimated at 90 million acres. It was probably inconceivable to most people at the time that this enormous supply of wood someday could be consumed and result in a landscape of devastated forests.

From the colonial period until the start of the Civil War, farmers throughout the southeastern Coastal Plain and Piedmont cleared forests for crop production. By 1860, in Virginia, more than 25 million acres, nearly half of the land, had been cleared. Soil erosion became a major problem, and by the end of the Civil War, declining soil productivity led farmers to abandon large amounts of land throughout the Southeastern United States (Fox and others 2007).

After the Civil War, the South's economy was in shambles and forested land was inexpensive. Northern industrialists purchased timberland and hired local labor to operate large sawmills, particularly in the Mid-South. While resulting in deforestation throughout the South, the massive harvesting of the South's virgin forests nevertheless provided a basis for economic recovery of the South.

Railroads played a large role in the South's forests. Their expansion across the country in the 1880s made it easy for people to move into the Great Plains and West, thereby feeding great need for building materials for new homes and businesses. At the same time, railroads, along with steam-powered logging and milling equipment, brought to the South the technology to quickly harvest and mill tremendous quantities of timber. Logging and milling took place mainly in the western portion of the Gulf Coastal Plain where virgin pine forests had remained largely untouched.

Virgin longleaf pines near Flatwoods, LA, typical of the old-growth forests in the West Gulf Region. Photograph is circa late 1940s.

This Southern Forest Experiment Station building at the Stuart Nursery served as an office and laboratory for Station employees assigned to the nursery in the mid-1930s.

Cutover conditions like those in this photograph, taken on the Longleaf Tract of the Palustris Experimental Forest, were common across millions of acres in the West Gulf Coastal Plain in the 1930s and 1940s.

Philip C. Wakeley conducted reforestation research in 1935 at the Stuart Nursery.

Wakeley (1954) stated that there were 13 million acres of forest land in the South that needed to be planted. Later, Wahlenberg (1960) estimated that 29 million acres were in need of reforestation. These conditions resulted from abusive agricultural practices that degraded soil productivity and from exploitative timber harvesting without provision for regeneration.

Reforestation techniques became a high priority for Southern Forest Experiment Station scientists. Philip C. Wakeley was assigned responsibility for reforestation research when he reported to work for the Southern

Station in 1924. His early nursery research was done in collaboration with the Great Southern Lumber Company in Bogalusa, LA. The lumber company had begun nursery development in the early 1920s under the direction of J.K. Johnson, the company's practical forester, and F.O. (Red) Bateman, the company's head ranger. Bateman and Wakeley developed early nursery and planting practices that landowners across the South adopted and applied. Wakeley's collaboration with the Great Southern Lumber Company ended in the early 1930s when the company went into receivership due to economic pressures of the Great Depression and because of diminishing amounts of old-growth timber.

The Southern Station's reforestation research moved to the Stuart Nursery established by the Kisatchie National Forest near Pollock in central Louisiana. The Stuart Nursery, established in 1934, was supported by a Civilian Conservation Corps camp that provided much of the needed technical support. The Southern Station developed an office and a laboratory at the nursery where assigned scientists worked under Wakeley's direction.

Establishment of the Palustris Experimental Forest

Moving the Southern Station's reforestation research to the Stuart Nursery required a field laboratory to serve as an outplanting site for evaluating the effectiveness of proposed nursery practices. In 1934, Philip Wakeley prepared documentation to establish the Palustris Experimental Forest, and its establishment was formally approved in 1935.

J.K. Johnson Tract

The newly created Palustris Experimental Forest consisted of 2,030 acres of cutover (completely harvested) longleaf pine forest type about 20 miles southwest of Alexandria, LA. The name Palustris was chosen because it is the scientific name for longleaf pine (*Pinus palustris*), the species in the greatest need for reforestation technology.

J.K. Johnson, chief forester for the Great Southern Lumber Company.

Well before its establishment as an experimental forest, the Palustris originally supported a heavy stand of pure longleaf pine (Wakeley 1954). Around 1907, a portion of the longleaf pine forests was logged with teams of oxen, and in 1917, the remainder of the forests was cleared with steam skidders. Subsequently, except for a few residual longleaf pines scattered and in clumps, the forest was open grassland with little natural longleaf reproduction. Fire protection was lacking until the late 1920s and imperfect until 1933. Fire and hog protection were fairly effective from 1934, when experimental planting began, until 1941, when many of the country's resources were diverted from domestic uses to military ones in support of World War II.

In 1946, the protection and use of the Palustris Experimental Forest was restored, and the tract still is used as a resource for many and varied research programs. This portion of the experimental forest was named the J.K. Johnson Tract in 1950 when the Longleaf Tract was added to the forest. This part of the Experimental Forest was named in recognition of J.K. Johnson, the first forester hired by the Great Southern Lumber Company.

Johnson had no forestry education but great practical experience, and led the early reforestation efforts of the Great Southern. Hired by Great Southern Lumber Company in 1920, Johnson came to be called the earliest industrial forester in the South (Campbell 1976). Johnson's support of reforestation was critical for the continuing and strong collaboration in the 1920s between Great Southern Lumber Company and the Southern Forest Experiment Station.

Longleaf Tract

In 1944 and 1945, Robert S. Campbell of the Southern Station in New Orleans started studies in forest grazing (Cassady and Mann 1954). Much of the Johnson Tract was committed to reforestation studies—more than 750 acres were in plantings of nursery studies. Many of these plantations were used for studies of thinning methods and other management techniques. Additional sites for range and other long-term research were needed to address issues related to forest grazing, forest range improvement, and use of chemicals to control scrub oaks. In 1950, the Longleaf Tract, an area of 5,800 acres, was purchased and added to the Palustris Experimental Forest. Much like the Johnson Tract area, the Longleaf Tract was a cutover longleaf pine site, primarily with blue-stem grass (*Andropogon gerardii* and *Schizachyrium scoparium* species) ground cover suitable for livestock grazing.

Outside the southern boundary of the Kisatchie National Forest when purchased, the Longleaf Tract was added to Kisatchie National Forest landholdings for management purposes. The Longleaf Tract is near McNary, LA, about 15 miles from the Johnson Tract.

Forest Administrators

For many years, the J.K. Johnson Tract and the Longleaf Tract were run as distinct entities from one another, meaning that each tract was overseen by its own manager. Even with this requirement of management staffing, relatively few scientists have managed the Palustris Experimental Forest during its 75 years of existence.

Philip C. Wakeley

A 1924 graduate of Cornell University, Philip Wakeley was responsible for establishing the Palustris Experimental Forest in 1935. He also managed the J.K. Johnson Tract until the end of World War II. In the late 1930s, Wakeley, with help from Civilian Conservation Corps crews, planted about 750,000 seedlings on the Johnson Tract in reforestation studies (Wakeley and Barnett 2011). Data from these studies became an important resource for his "Planting the Southern Pines" (Wakeley 1954), which, along with an earlier version (Wakeley 1935), provided guidelines for establishing southern pine plantations across the South. During World War II, no resources were available to maintain or even protect these studies, and forest management on the Johnson Tract necessarily languished until 1946.

Wakeley also was responsible for establishing early tree improvement and genetics efforts with southern pine species. His efforts were instrumental in demonstrating the potential benefits of genetics programs. The Palustris Experimental Forest served as a significant resource for much of this early effort.

John T. Cassady

John Cassady was named officer-in-charge for the Alexandria Research Center when it was created in 1946, and his responsibilities included supervision of the Palustris Experimental Forest. Trained at the University of Arizona and a former lieutenant colonel in the U.S. Army Air Corps, Cassady was more aligned with range management issues than forest management. Because open grazing of cattle, sheep, and hogs on cutover land impeded reforestation efforts, range management was a major concern. Range studies led by Robert S. Campbell—begun in 1944 on the Kisatchie National Forest's Chandler Tract near Dry Prong, LA—became the basis for this program of research at the Alexandria Research Center.

R.S. Campbell and John Cassady measuring samples of forage produced under varying overstory conditions.

Cassady followed up on the range studies. He promoted creating the Longleaf Tract portion of the Experimental Forest to provide enhanced capability for grazing studies. The Longleaf Tract was established in 1950 to develop better methods of planting and growing longleaf pine and to conduct research into increasing beef production on pine forest ranges without damage to the timber crop.

In 1951, William F. Mann, Jr., was transferred to the Alexandria Research Center to head timber management research programs, when a number of other scientists were added to the center's staff to work on a significant multidisciplinary research effort.

One of Cassady's strengths was his ability to bring together State and Federal agencies, private industries, and others for work on the research of the Alexandria Center. Through collaboration with the Southern Forest Experiment Station, Roy O. Martin Lumber Co., and the Louisiana Forestry Commission, residential and supporting structures were built on the Longleaf Tract in 1953. In 1956, Cassady transferred to head the Southeastern Forest Experiment Station's range program at Fort Myers, FL.

William F. (Bill) Mann, Jr.

Bill Mann replaced Cassady as leader of the Alexandria Research Center. Mann had forestry training at Pennsylvania State University and experience from other research locations. With increasing funding and cooperation from other organizations, the Alexandria Research Center significantly expanded its professional staff. Research widened to include seed physiology, direct seeding, nursery culture, soil relations, plantation establishment and management, range management, chemical control of hardwoods, forest insects, wildlife, and tree improvement. Mann built collaborative relationships with organizations that developed political influence, resulting in Congressional support that funded excellent new facilities in Pineville, LA, in 1963.

Bill Mann built collaboration with Federal, State, and private organizations that led to excellent facilities and research programs.

When the Forest Service reorganized it's research initiatives in 1964, Alexandria Research Center programs were completely restructured. The center's large program of many disciplines of research was divided into a number of smaller projects with much narrower research aims. Mann was named project leader for Timber Management Research (TMR), the largest of the new research work units. Other projects were Forest Insect Research, Forest Range Research, Forest Products Research, and Forest Fire Research.

In the TMR project's purview were reforestation (e.g., seed physiology, nursery production and direct seeding), competition control, soil-related issues, plantation growth and yield, tree improvement, and related silvicultural research.

In 1969, a portion of Mann's TMR program was withdrawn to create an Intensive Culture Research Project, with assigned programs including techniques to maximize stand productivity with a focus on fertilization, irrigation, soil management, and post-planting competition control. This unit was led by Eugene Shoulders.

During Mann's tenure as leader of TMR, the unit gained regional, national, and international recognition for productivity and significant research accomplishments.

The research center received the U.S. Department of Agriculture (USDA) Superior Service Award in 1961 for contributions in direct seeding, chemical competition control, and range management research. Scientists from many parts of the world came to Pineville to study the project's research accomplishments.

Mann died on the job in 1980 while evaluating a study site in the Kisatchie National Forest.

Vince L. Duvall

Vince Duvall joined the Southern Station to lead range research on the Palustris Experimental Forest in 1959. During the research reorganization of 1964, he was named project leader for Forest Range Research. Duvall assumed administrative responsibility for the Longleaf Tract of the Palustris Experimental Forest while Mann retained responsibility for the Johnson Tract. Duvall came to the Southern Station a mature scientist and quickly developed meaningful research programs that built on the ongoing efforts in range management.

Duvall built a small but well-trained staff of botanists and range specialists. Considerable scientific effort went into understanding forage plants, their seasonal availability and their nutritional value. From this information, researchers developed supplemental winter feeding guidelines. This range program was designed to support grazing under forested conditions, but as forest stands developed, the availability of forage declined. Researchers began working with cooperating cattlemen

Vince L. Duvall (left) with U.S. Senator Allen Ellender, long-time chair of the U.S. Senate's Agriculture Committee, at a field day held for Ellender. Whit Whitaker (right) was the first range technician hired by the Southern Station at the Alexandria Forestry Center.

on recommendations for the level of tree stocking that was compatible with sustainable levels of forage production.

Duvall served as project leader and administrator of the Longleaf Tract until 1968 when he was transferred to an assistant director position in New Orleans.

Henry A. Pearson

Henry Pearson accepted leadership of the range research unit in 1969 and expanded the role of the Palustris Experimental Forest to include evaluating the interrelationships among the South's livestock, trees, and wildlife. Cattle had grazed on the Longleaf Tract, both before and after the designation of Palustris as an experimental forest. Under Pearson's leadership, the research program on the Longleaf Tract began to provide land managers with alternatives for attaining multiple-use objectives. Research provided data to quantify the effects of livestock and timber management practices on trees, forage, livestock, watershed, and wildlife. In-depth ecological relationships and descriptions for forest-range management practices were based on an understanding of overstory tree, understory herbage and browse relationships, and forage responses to direct-seeded and planted pines, prescribed burning, and livestock grazing.

Henry A. Pearson, a noted leader in conducting and transferring range research results.

As both economics of grazing cattle under forested conditions and availability of open forest lands declined, Pearson led a shift in the range program to embrace a broader agroforestry context. His research on the Palustris Experimental Forest pioneered dual land use with livestock and trees in the South, leading to better wildlife habitat as well as increased food and fiber supplies for commercial use.

The range-related studies on the Palustris Experimental Forest focused on an array of interacting resource values long before there was emphasis to do so. These studies provided a vital link in multiple-use management of natural resources throughout the South, providing much of the ecological basis for managing multiple resources on both governmental and private lands. One highlight

of this effort was the pooling of research information at a 1987 workshop, culminating with the publication of "Ecological, Physical, and Socioeconomic Relationships within Southern National Forests" (Pearson and others 1987).

Pearson's tenure as leader of the range program between 1969 and 1991 was interrupted for 2 years (1976-77) while he served as branch chief for Range, Wildlife, and Fish Habitat Research in the Forest Service's Washington Office. During this period, Warren P. Clary served as project leader for the range program. Clary was a range specialist from the Rocky Mountain Forest Experiment Station and returned to a position there in 1977.

International involvement characterized Pearson's leadership. In 1974, he represented the U.S. Department of Agriculture at the 12th International Grassland Congress in Moscow, Russia, presenting research findings from the Longleaf Tract. His presentation was well received, and he participated in most grassland congresses since around the world. Compared to range programs in the Western United States, range programs in the Southern United States were small, but Pearson represented the Southern Station and the Forest Service well internationally.

The range program was closed by the Southern Forest Experiment Station in 1991 as a result of budgetary limitations and shifts in program emphases. Pearson was a creative and energetic leader, and was highly regarded by land managers across the South. When the program closed, Pearson transferred to a similar position in the U.S. Department of Agriculture, Agricultural Research Service in Booneville, AR, where he developed an agroforestry research program. Management of the Longleaf Tract moved back to the Forest Management Research program.

James P. (Jim) Barnett

Jim Barnett began his research career at the Alexandria Research Center in 1961 after release from active duty in the U.S. Coast Guard Reserve. He was assigned to southern pine seed research in Mann's Timber Management Research program. After Mann's death in 1980, Barnett was named project leader of the Timber Management Research unit, where he managed the J.K. Johnson Tract. In 1992, after the closure of the range program, he was assigned the additional responsibility of managing the Longleaf Tract. He continued with these responsibilities until he retired in 2005.

The Palustris Experimental Forest became a site for much of Barnett's research in southern pine reforestation. A seed-testing laboratory was housed on the Johnson Tract until new facilities were built in Pineville, LA. Studies related to direct seeding and planting were conducted there as well. In the early 1970s, Barnett began researching the technology of growing seedlings in containers, work that supports current reforestation methodology for longleaf pines.

Jim Barnett's reforestation research over 40 years has shaped plantation establishment technology used across the South.

During more than 40 years at the Alexandria Forestry Center, Barnett advanced basic and applied knowledge about successful techniques for seed physiology, nursery practices, and reforestation worldwide. He received national recognition from the Chief of the Forest Service, the Secretary of Agriculture, and the Society of American Foresters. In addition, he participated in scientific exchanges with more than a dozen countries and made a number of international keynote addresses. With more than 300 publications related to reforestation of southern pine species, he helped shape the current southern pine plantation establishment technology that is applied across the South.

In addition to his personal research, Barnett led a productive research work unit that provided critical information for establishing and managing southern pine plantations. The research program's focus areas include over- and under-story plant competition, stand growth and yield prediction models, soil-site relationships, fire effects on stand management, and physiology of silvicultural practices.

Barnett led the development of the Forest Service's National Reforestation, Nurseries, and Genetic Resources (RNGR) program, which emerged in response to a loss, across the Forest Service, of technical expertise in reforestation. Supported by Forest Service branches (State and Private Forestry, Research and Development, and National Forest System), the program addresses forestry and conservation land management issues and wildland restoration. An important aspect of the RNGR program was an outreach program to Native Americans.

James D. (Dave) Haywood

Dave Haywood joined the Timber Management Project in 1978 as a silviculturist. His research has focused on the ecology and management of the longleaf pine ecosystem. Even before taking over management of the Palustris Experimental Forest, he was assigned the responsibility of coordinating with the Kisatchie National Forest on thinning and harvesting activities and on the scheduling of prescribed burning. Haywood is recognized as one of the premier silviculturists of the longleaf pine ecosystem. His research on longleaf pine regeneration and restoration has covered the influences of vegetation control, fertilization, prescribed fire, and pine straw harvesting on long-term productivity and stability of plant communities of the longleaf pine ecosystem. He also has published widely on the management of loblolly pine (*Pinus taeda*) stands, especially on the effects of thinning on growth and yield of young plantations as well as on the effects of harvesting and regeneration practices on the productivity of pine stands in the next rotation.

Dave Haywood assumed management responsibility of the Palustris Experiment Forest in 2005.

After Jim Barnett's retirement, the Pineville forest management research program was reorganized. The unit's project leader, Kristina F. Connor, is stationed in Auburn, AL. To meet the need for local management of the Palustris Experimental Forest, Haywood was assigned administrative responsibility for both tracts. In this role, he has built an excellent relationship with the managers of the Kisatchie National Forest that is essential for the protection and management of the experimental forest.

Research Programs

Through the 75 years of its existence, the Palustris Experimental Forest has served as a resource for conducting many and varied research programs designed to restore the South's devastated forests and enhance their productivity. The list of research efforts is long, and documentation of some programs is limited. It is possible, then, to focus only on major research initiatives.

Cassady and Mann (1954) document well the conditions in the South in the late 1940s and early 1950s that required a major research initiative. The forests of Louisiana and east Texas, in particular, were devastated by aggressive harvesting. About 20 percent of the forest land, or 1,250,000 acres, had been clearcut so completely that it was barren of trees and in need of artificial regeneration. Another 3 million acres of timberland were producing much below full potential because scrub oaks and other low-value hardwoods were overabundant and pine stands were inadequate. The cutover pine lands supported an abundant stand of native grasses, and range livestock grazing became an important industry. Grazing was mostly on the free-range principle. Most of the land was unfenced, and all kinds, grades, and ownership of stock grazed together. The Alexandria Research Center was established in 1946 to develop improved methods of reforestation and management with the aim of guiding forest landowners in the task of attaining optimum production and income. Initially, five lines of investigation were selected:

1. Reforesting cutover pine lands.
2. Managing pine plantations for optimum returns.
3. Controlling low-grade hardwoods with chemicals.
4. Improving management of livestock and forage on forest ranges.
5. Determining costs and returns of good forest management.

Programs were established to address these research needs, and periodically the research programs were reevaluated and modified to meet new developments and program needs. The Palustris Experimental Forest became a field laboratory for developing and evaluating ongoing research programs in reforestation and management of southern pine plantations.

Because of open range laws, livestock was to allowed to graze on unfenced, cutover land that had been planted to pine.

Forest Management

The early emphasis of research on the Palustris Experimental Forest was called timber management. In the 1980s, the name for the emphasis switched to forest management to suggest a broader context of management objectives. Much of the forest management research undertaken on the Palustris Experimental Forest is described in the following sections.

Artificial Regeneration

Natural regeneration on cutover lands was limited by the scarcity of remnant stands or seed trees. Artificial regeneration, then, became a critical research area in restoring the South's forests. However, the supply of quality seed was insufficient to support the regeneration effort. Seed research was initiated to address this problem.

Seed research—Wakeley's "Planting the Southern Pines" (1954) provided considerable information on collecting and producing pine seeds for nursery use. It was difficult to produce and store enough longleaf pine seeds for planting, and research concentrated on how to quantify collecting, processing, storing, and treating procedures. In the late 1950s, B.F. (Bob) McLemore, recruited to address seed problems, started seed storage evaluations and a wide range of seed physiology studies. He was joined in the effort in 1961 with the assignment of Jim Barnett to the project. Under the team of McLemore and Barnett, seed physiology research was expanded to all four major pines and those minor species of pines that have a range in the South.

Early seed studies were conducted in a seed testing laboratory on the experimental forest. With construction of the Alexandria Forestry Center facilities in 1963, testing moved there. Seed collecting, processing, and storing studies continued on the experimental forest.

This seed research is reported in many publications, including research on collection and processing (Barnett 1976a, 1988, McLemore 1959, Pawuk and Barnett 1979), storage (Barnett 1969, 1970, Barnett and McLemore 1970, Barnett and Vozzo 1985, McLemore and Barnett 1966), dormancy (Barnett 1972, 1976b, Barnett and McLemore 1984), and seed treatments (Barnett 1971, Barnett and McGilvray 2002a, McLemore 1971, McLemore and Czabator 1961).

McLemore was transferred to the Southern Forest Experiment Station's research work unit in Monticello, AR, in 1978, but Barnett continued seed research specifically related to nursery problems until his retirement in 2005.

TOP: Bob McLemore removing seeds from cold storage for testing.
BOTTOM: A germinating longleaf pine seed.

Seed research was critical to successful artificial regeneration programs across the South—where more than 1 billion southern pine seedlings are produced annually—as well as in many countries where southern pines have been introduced.

Direct seeding—In the late 1940s, researchers estimated that it would take 50 years to reforest the treeless longleaf pine land of Louisiana and east Texas if nursery seedlings were planted at the then-current rate (Cassady and Mann 1954). Direct seeding promised to be cheaper, faster, and more effective than planting, and its development became a priority of the Alexandria Research Center. Early on, researchers understood that major failures of longleaf

Flocks of Eastern Meadowlarks ate large quantities of seeds.

pines to seed could be attributed to predation by birds and rodents. Harold J. Derr became leader of this research initiative. He and Bill Mann, the Center Leader, got Brooke Meanley of the U.S. Fish and Wildlife Service to help them evaluate potential animal repellents (Mann and others 1956).

In a number of studies on the Palustris Experimental Forest, a chemical mixture of thiram (as bird repellent) and endrin (as a rodent repellent) was found to be effective in protecting the seeds from predation (Derr 1964).

During the 1960s and 1970s, direct seeding was used to reforest hundreds of thousands of acres of cutover land in the West Gulf Region. This technology was extended to other regions of the country, as well as internationally. Seeding, which works well where large areas need reforestation, has been used effectively following large wildfires. Aerial application was the most efficient method of seeding, but it often resulted in overstocked stands. To better control tree spacing, row and hand seeding were then developed and worked well for smaller tracts of land. These techniques are described in Derr and Mann's "Direct-seeding Pines of the South" (1971).

Development of direct seeding was one of the major accomplishments that led to the research unit receiving the USDA Superior Service award in 1961. Large acreages of cutover land were reforested. But direct seeding fell into disfavor due to lack of stocking control and less consistent establishment success. There was also concern that endrin entering streamways might be toxic to fish. Under a U.S. Department of Agriculture reevaluation of such chemicals in the mid-1970s, Barnett led a multi-agency team that helped determine the relative safety of endrin to the environment in small applications (Barnett and others 1980). Barnett also helped lead a search for a replacement for endrin, and

TOP: *Harold J. Derr sowing longleaf seeds with a cyclone seeder.*
BOTTOM: *Tommy Rhame, first technician on the Palustris Experimental Forest, supervised and trained a core group of technicians who spent their careers supporting research programs.*

with other researchers found that the most promising chemical, when used with thiram, is capsicum, a concentrated hot pepper sauce (Nolte and Barnett 2000).

Direct seeding was a major advance in the reforestation of millions of acres of open cutover land. It is rarely used today because conditions where it is best applied are now infrequently encountered. (Direct seeding works best on large open areas where competition control can be readily applied and where areas are large enough so seed predator populations from surrounding areas do not overwhelm repellent effectiveness.)

Bareroot nursery research—The Palustris Experimental Forest was established in 1935 to provide an experimental area to study the bareroot nursery procedures under development at the Kisatchie National Forest's Stuart Nursery. With assistance from Civilian Conservation Corps crews, nearly 750,000 seedlings were planted in studies on the experimental forest. The bareroot nursery research shaped Wakeley's "Planting the Southern Pines" (1954), a publication vital to the effective application of artificial regeneration and which, while long out of print, is still relied on as a solid reference on the seedling physiology of southern pines.

Studies continued at the Stuart Nursery until it was closed in the mid-1960s. A small nursery was established on the Johnson Tract to evaluate the effectiveness of seed treatments, and after the small nursery closed in the late 1960s, nursery research was mostly limited to studies of seed treatments for optimizing germination and early seedling development in nurseries.

William H. Pawuk, a plant pathologist funded by the Southern Region in Atlanta, GA, was added to the nursery research program in 1974 and nursery research again surged. In the early 1980s, John C. Brissette replaced Pawuk, and, in collaboration with

the National Forest System and State and Private Forestry specialists, helped bring the bareroot nursery program back into a leadership role in the South. A collaborative Reforestation Improvement Program was established to improve the quality of seedlings produced in all of the Forest Service's nurseries. The goal was to apply the best known seedling physiology technology to all Forest Service nurseries and quantify results (Owsten and others 1990a). The Palustris Experimental Forest was an outplanting site for many study evaluations.

Longleaf pine continued to have the primary reforestation need. But difficulty in obtaining reforestation success on an operational scale resulted in expanded research that focused on optimizing seed and nursery practices for other southern pines. An example of this was the cooperative effort to improve establishment success of planted shortleaf pine (*Pinus echinata*).

Silviculturists from the Ouachita and Ozark National Forests approached unit scientists to help improve establishment success of shortleaf pine in the mountains of Arkansas and Oklahoma. In the early 1980s, first-year survival of planted shortleaf pine was less than 50 percent. As a result of these discussions, a Shortleaf Pine Artificial Regeneration task force was established to focus on the problems. It was led by Jim Barnett and John Brissette and involved other specialists from the Forest Service, Weyerhaeuser

This small experimental forest nursery at the J.K. Johnson Tract headquarters site was used to evaluate effects of seed treatments.

Company, Arkansas Forestry Commission, and Louisiana and Oklahoma State Universities and University of Arkansas at Monticello. During a 5-year period beginning in 1985, about 15 studies were conducted, including evaluations of seed treatments (Barnett 1993), stock types (Barnett and Brissette 2004), nursery studies to improve seedling quality (Brissette and Carlson 1987), use of fungicides to reduce seedling storage pathogens (Barnett and others 1988), use of root growth potential to identify optimum seedling lifting-date windows (Hallgren and Tauer 1989), studies to relate seedling physiology and morphology to performance under stressful conditions (Sword and others 2005), and evaluation of post-planting competition control on seedling survival and growth (Yeiser and Barnett 1991).

John C. Brissette was selected as a project leader in the Northern Research Station.

When the results of these studies were implemented, operational planting survival of shortleaf pine in mountainous conditions increased to about 85 percent (Barnett and Brissette 2007, Brissette and Barnett 1992). The 1989 decision to cease clearcutting on the Ouachita and Ozark National Forests greatly diminished the need for shortleaf pine reforestation technology.

John Brissette transferred to a leadership position in the Northeastern Forest Experiment Station in the early 1990s. Thus ended a 20-year relationship during which the Southern Region funded a reforestation position in the research unit. Another opportunity occurred, however, to maintain and enhance the unit's nursery-related programs.

In the mid-1990s, in response to loss of technical expertise across Forest Service programs, several parties—State and Private Forestry's Cooperative Forestry, National Forest System's Forest and Range Management, and Research and Development's Southern Research Station—joined in supporting a national specialist in nursery and reforestation issues. Internationally renowned Richard W. (Dick) Tinus was assigned to the Forest Management Research Work Unit in Pineville to carry out this responsibility.

Early into the effort, Tinus' untimely death required the Southern Station to recruit a replacement. R. Kasten (Kas) Dumroese of the University of Idaho was subsequently attached to the Pineville unit (while stationed in Moscow, ID), and he soon was recognized for his technical ability, productivity, and leadership skills.

Kas Dumroese serves as national nursery specialist for the Reforestation, Nursery, and Genetic Resources program.

This collaborative effort was formalized in 2003 with the signing of a Forest Service-wide Memorandum of Understanding to establish the National Center for Reforestation, Nursery, and Genetic Resources (RNGR). The informal RNGR program had gained national attention for its productivity and effectiveness, and became known for its work in providing nursery and restoration technology to Native American governments.

RNGR staff understood that full appreciation of American Indian culture and beliefs regarding plants meant recruiting help from someone who understood tribal culture. RNGR brought in an American Indian from the Navajo tribe—Jeremiah R. (Jeremy) Pinto—to serve as a tribal nursery coordinator. Pinto brought an unusual capability to communicate well with tribal members, as well as with more traditional nursery managers.

Dumroese and Pinto expanded the customary nursery meeting with tribal workshops that addressed needs of tribal members, and, along with other researchers, published tribal nursery manuals on native plants of tribal interest (Dumroese and others 2009, Landis and others 2005, Luna and others 2003).

Jeremy Pinto, tribal nursery coordinator for the Reforestation, Nursery, and Genetic Resources program.

The RNGR program has been successful, boasting an exceptional record of relevant publications, including a number of publication series, e.g., Native Plants Journal (www.nativeplantnetwork.org) (information on a wide array of native plants with propagation guidelines); Container Tree Nursery Manual (seven volumes of detailed information about production of container tree seedlings); Forest Nursery Notes (updates on recent publications and meetings that support nursery specialists); National Proceedings, Forest and Conservation Nursery Associations (combined proceedings of regional nursery meetings); and Tree Planters' Notes (updates on forest tree seedling production). These publications are available through the RNGR Web site: www.rngr net.

Other researchers provide nursery, reforestation, and genetics guidelines for both national and international managers, e.g., Dumroese and others 2005, Dumroese and others 2008, and Landis and others 2009.

After Barnett's retirement as project leader of the Forest Management Research Unit in 2005, Dumroese and Pinto were eventually attached to the Rocky Mountain Research Station.

Container seedling production—In the early 1970s, growing container tree seedlings for reforestation began in Canada and the Pacific Northwest where establishment of many species of bareroot nursery stock was difficult and expensive. Most southern nursery specialists questioned the need to grow southern pine seedlings in containers for a couple of good reasons; for one, the costs would be considerably more than for bareroot stock; and for another, bareroot seedlings of most species could be established successfully. Most agreed, however, that container seedling production of southern pines should be evaluated. As a result, Barnett, of the Pineville Forest Management Research Unit, undertook development of container seedling protocols for southern pines.

When container research began, numerous types of containers were being considered and about 30 were evaluated in trials established on the Johnson Tract. Eventually, the plug-type container was found most effective because this type permitted rapid egress of roots into the soil (Barnett and McGilvray 1981, 1997).

During a 25-year period, studies were installed to evaluate factors such as seedling density and age (Barnett 1980), mycorrhizal effects (Barnett 1983, Pawuk and Barnett 1981, Ruehle and others 1981), seedling physiology (Barnett 1984), seed quality and sowing rate (Barnett and McGilvray 2002a), and comparisons with bareroot stock (Barnett and McGilvray 1993, South and Barnett 1986, South and others 2005). Several

John M. McGilvray, nursery research technician, inspecting a planted container seedling.

publications compiling recommendations and workshop proceedings provided information to user groups (Barnett and Brissette 1986, Barnett and others 2002a, Barnett and McGilvray 1997, Brissette and others 1991, Guldin and Barnett 1982).

Container nursery technology was slow to gain acceptance in the South. Costs were at least twice that of bareroot stock, and seedlings of most southern species survive well after planting. (The exception is longleaf pine, which generally has poor outplanting success.) Despite the poor outplanting performance of bareroot longleaf pine, few professionals considered using container longleaf pine seedlings. This changed dramatically in the late 1990s when interest in restoring longleaf pine increased significantly, particularly in the Southeast, where Federal incentive programs favored planting of longleaf pine.

Demand for container stock increased dramatically, and because resources to establish container nurseries were small compared to bareroot nurseries, hundreds of small "mom and pop" nurseries, sprung up across the South using published techniques (Barnett and McGilvray 1997). With acceptance of container stock planting for

Jim Barnett led development of seed and container production.

longleaf pine restoration, the need to establish seedling specifications for container nursery stock became critical. Interim seedling specifications were developed and published (Barnett and others 2002b, Dumroese and others 2009).

Annual production of longleaf seedlings in containers increased from about 7 million in 1984 to about 75 million in 2008. Almost all nursery production of longleaf pine is now in containers.

Control of undesired hardwoods

An immediate research need noted in the late 1940s (when the Alexandria Research Center was established) was development of chemical treatments for controlling low-grade hardwoods (Cassady and Mann 1954). Much of the forest land in the West Gulf Region not completely

devoid of trees was covered with non-merchantable hardwoods, and removal of these hardwoods was critical for restoring productive pine forests.

Fred A. Peevy, the first employee of the Alexandria Research Center in 1946, was responsible for developing chemical control techniques for these low-quality upland hardwoods—primarily blackjack oak (*Quercus marilandica*), post oak (*Q. stellata*), red oak (*Q. falcata*), sweetgum (*Liquidambar styraciflua*), and hickory (*Carya sp.*). Ammate® was a known chemical that would kill trees if applied in notches cut around the tree. Peevy worked with this chemical and refined its application techniques (Peevy 1947). His early research established him as the expert in herbicide control of woody plants, and he began a process of evaluating the efficacy of new chemicals as they became available.

Ammate® was soon replaced by agricultural weed killers 2,4-D and 2,4,5-T. Peevy's research developed application rates and methodology for these chemicals that became the mainstay forestry treatment for a number of years (Peevy 1960, 1961). As environmental problems became evident with these chemicals, Peevy evaluated a number of newer and safer products and developed recommendations for using them to control a range of upland hardwood species.

Applying Ammate® by the "hack and squirt" technique.

Fred A. Peevy applying chemical basal spray to a blackjack oak.

15

Peevy's research established the Alexandria Research Center as leader in the effort to control undesired woody species that, if left unchecked, would limit reforestation of vast acreages of cutover pine timberland. Individual tree application by tree injectors and stand application by aerial spraying and mist blowing became accepted methodologies for controlling an array of woody-plant species. Peevy did pioneering research that led to the restoration of large areas of pine forests. His research on the control of hardwood species in pine plantations was recognized in 1961 with the USDA Superior Service Award.

Late in Peevy's career, a decision was made to expand the nature of herbicide research by adding a plant physiologist—Homer A. Brady joined the staff in the late 1960s. His basic research examined the methodologies of chemical action and how they were affected by environmental conditions (Brady 1975, Brady and Hall 1976). Joining Brady in a professional support position was Oscar Hall, a graduate of Tuskegee Institute and likely the Southern Station's earliest African American scientist (Hall 1973). Brady left the research group in the late 1970s and Thomas E. (Tucker) Campbell assumed responsibility for woody-plant herbicide research until the early 1980s, when the research program was transferred to the Southern Station's Auburn, AL, research unit. Hall transferred to the Wind River Nursery in Washington as a nursery specialist. Thus, a long and productive line of research that had a major impact on reforestation of the South's cutover forests ended.

Oscar Hall, one of the Southern Station's earliest African American scientists.

Although primary woody-plant herbicide research was transferred to the Auburn unit, application of chemicals to reduce grass and forb competition remained with the Pineville unit. Longleaf pine reforestation requires some control of competition, particularly while seedlings are in the grass stage. Dave Haywood has conducted silvicultural research on methodologies to limit competition during pine seedling establishment. This research is discussed in the Competition Control with Herbicides section under Stand Management Studies.

Tree improvement and genetics

Tree improvement and genetics research on the Palustris Experimental Forest began with one longleaf pine seedling; but it was a special seedling that was found healthy in an abandoned nursery bed overcome by brown-spot needle disease (*Mycosphaerella dearneii*) (syn. *Scirrhia acicola*). Brown-spot needle disease defoliates seedlings, delaying their emergence from the grass stage, and often resulting in seedling mortality.

Paul V. Siggers, the pathologist for the Southern Forest Experiment Station who described and named the disease (Siggers 1932), recognized the significance of the healthy seedling and transplanted it on the Palustris Experimental Forest in 1937. The seedling developed into a brown-spot resistant tree and became a source of genetic material in a program to develop a disease-resistant strain of longleaf pine.

The uniqueness of the tree and its potential for reducing infection from brown-spot disease resulted it being named "Father Abraham" or "Abe" to reflect the potential for developing a long line of disease-resistant trees.

Once Abe began flowering, Harold J. Derr began studies to evaluate disease resistance by selfing and cross-pollinating, and demonstrated that resistance is heritable (Derr and Melder 1970). Derr began a process to evaluate more than 900 superior-tree selections from the southern national forest tree improvement program, working with the idea that disease resistance resulted in better seedling survival and superior growth. Through this process, the incorporation of Abe's pollen in the pollination mix generally increased resistance and seedling performance (Derr and Melder 1970).

Evaluations of disease resistance were made on the Longleaf Tract, where there was a moderate to severe brown-spot hazard. Seedlings were planted in shallow furrows to ensure exposure to the disease's fungal spores from rain splash. Because the Longleaf Tract was a cutover longleaf pine site, many seedlings had remained in the grass stage for years and spores from these seedlings became a source for continuing inoculation. Brown-spot needle disease is now less of a problem; sites where inoculum develops—sites with abundant seedlings remaining in the grass stage—now are seldom encountered.

Derr, in collaboration with E. Bayne Snyder of the Southern Institute of Forest Genetics at Gulfport, MS, published review papers on the genetics of longleaf pine and its resistance to brown-spot needle disease (Snyder and Derr 1972, Snyder and others 1977).

A tree named "Abe," a brown-spot disease resistant longleaf pine about 35 years after planting on the experimental forest.

Derr also evaluated characteristics of hybrids of longleaf and slash (*Pinus elliottii*) pines. At 7 years old, these hybrids planted on the experimental forest demonstrated desirable characteristics of both parent species, closely resembling longleaf pine in form and branching habit but also beginning their height growth immediately. The hybrids appeared less susceptible than their parents to brown-spot needle blight of longleaf and fusiform rust of slash pine (Derr 1966).

Harold J. Derr (left) with Philip A. Briegleb, director of the Southern Station during the late 1950s and early 1960s, observing an outplanting of longleaf pine on the Longleaf Tract.

With Harold Derr's retirement in 1976, responsibility for tree improvement and genetics research was transferred to the Southern Institute of Forest Genetics. Abe, the brown-spot resistant longleaf tree, died in the early 1980s from a southern pine beetle infestation, although a number of clones from Abe had been created and remain on the experimental forest.

Soil-related programs

Soils and soil nutrient supply control the productivity of all our forests (Jokela and others 2010). Once an understanding of technology to reforest southern pines was developed, it became necessary to determine how varying soils and site conditions modified its application. Three major efforts were evaluated on the Palustris to determine the relation of soils types and their manipulation to pine plantation productivity: site preparation treatments, site-species studies, and a program to evaluate long-term soil productivity.

Site preparation treatments—Early site preparation studies primarily compared burning and mechanical treatments to unburned controls. Installed in the 1960s, these studies initially indicated improved growth of loblolly and slash pine from disking and mounding or bedding treatments (Mann and Derr 1970). However, after 10 years this initial growth advantage was lost. Even on poorly drained sites, bedding had no long-term benefit (Derr and Mann 1977, Haywood 1983, Lohrey 1974).

Disking and mounding upland sites, such as the site shown in the photograph, seldom results in a long-term improvement in growth regardless of species.

These and other studies showed that response to site preparation varies by species and soil type. Generally, however, mechanical treatments seemed to improve early performance by reducing competition and by incorporating nutrients in bedded planting spots. To better understand these relationships, Eugene (Gene) Shoulders installed a large study to evaluate species-site interactions (Shoulders 1976).

Site-species relationships—From 1954 to 1958, Gene Shoulders, with help of both public and private forestry organizations, established pine species comparisons on 113 uniform sites in Louisiana and Mississippi. Called the "choice of species study," three plots each of loblolly, slash, and longleaf pine were planted in a randomized block design on each location (Shoulders and Walker 1979). Shortleaf pine was included in about half of the installations where shortleaf pine was in its natural range. Early in the study, Shoulders classified the planting sites as wet, intermediate, or dry on the basis of soil classifications. Measurements were carried out during a 20-year period.

This huge study generated a number of findings (Shoulders 1983). First, neither longleaf nor shortleaf pine emerged as clearly superior to loblolly or slash pine for planting in Louisiana and portion of Mississippi represented by the study. Second, differences in planting

Gene Shoulders was an early advocate of applying soils knowledge to silviculture.

survival, fusiform rust infection, and fusiform induced mortality between loblolly and slash pine were seldom sufficient to cause one species to be favored over the other. Third, slash pine is a better choice than loblolly for planting on flat, wet sites having poorly drained soils. The two species performed equally well on intermediate and dry sites. Finally, chances for choosing the species best suited for planting on a particular site are improved if amount and seasonal distribution of rainfall, slope, and subsoil texture are considered in making the selection (Shoulders and Tiarks 1980b).

Longleaf pine compared poorly in this "choice of species" study due to poor planting technology for the species at the time of study installation. Shoulders (1985) built a case for longleaf by computing 20-year yields from current technology that allows longleaf to reach a height of 4 feet by the time it is 4 years old and that produces stocking equal to the other species. Based on these assumptions, potential yields of longleaf at 20 years equaled or exceeded that of loblolly in 97 percent of the installations.

Long-term soil productivity—A study on the Palustris forest reported by J.D. Haywood and A.E. Tiarks (1995) suggests that declining productivity of the next rotation may be caused by treatments meant to increase productivity in the present rotation. The authors compared burning only; burning and disking; and burning, disking and bedding for planting loblolly and slash pine. The study plantation was harvested after 22 years and replanted with the same species. The site was re-burned, but mechanical site preparation treatments were not repeated. After 10 years, standing volume in the second rotation was 55 and 38 percent below the first rotation for loblolly and slash pine, respectively.

This and similar studies worldwide prompted concern about the long-term effects of intensive stand management. In the United States, the Forest Service is mandated by law to sustain the inherent capacity of forest land it manages. To meet these requirements, land managers need valid soil-quality monitoring standards, and a national effort known as the Long-Term Soil Production (LTSP) program was initiated to establish these standards and provide a better understanding of the effects of organic matter removal and soil compaction—two effects linked to losses in soil productivity (Powers and others 1990).

The first of the LTSP program studies was an installation on the Longleaf Tract. The installation was organized and led by Allan Tiarks, soil scientist for the forest management research project. Tiarks established and implemented protocols used in the LTSP program, which included 12 additional installations in the South: three each on National Forests in Louisiana, Texas, Mississippi, and North Carolina (Tiarks and others 1990, 1992).

At each of the 13 sites, researchers applied three levels of compaction (none, moderate, severe) and three levels of organic matter removal (stem only, whole tree, and whole tree plus forest floor) in a factorial design. Half of each treatment plot was kept free from interspecies competition with herbicides (Scott and others 2004).

Soil compaction had no negative impacts on tree growth at 10 years; most sites responded positively to compaction due to the subsequent reduction of the shrub understory. Removing more organic matter than found in the stems reduced stand volume on eight of 10 sites by more than 15 percent.

This study indicates long-term soil productivity is negatively affected by harvesting operations that remove tree branches and foliage, and by site preparation operations that remove the forest floor, such as severe site preparation burns (Scott and others 2007).

In addition to the 13 study installations in the South, the LTSP program has been extended to locations throughout the United States and Canada (Fleming and

Intensive site preparation, such as this bedding treatment, has been determined to adversely affect stand productivity of some soils in the following rotation (Haywood and Tiarks 1995).

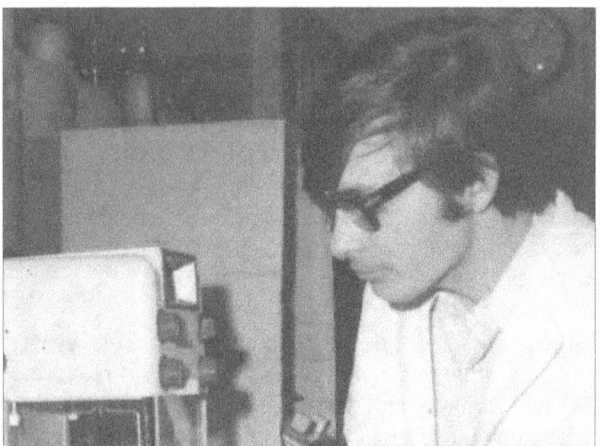

Allan E. Tiarks, early leader of Long-term Soil Productivity installations in the South, in the soils laboratory.

Andy Scott became leader of the international Long-term Soil Productivity program.

others 2006). The impetus for the LTSP study is the legal requirement that public lands are managed in ways that do not impair their long-term productivity.

Private landowners also need data on mitigative treatments for overcoming detrimental soil impacts as well as data on ameliorative treatments for increasing soil productivity.

To meet the need to complement and extend the LTSP program to industrial forests, a cooperative effort in 1993 brought together forest industries, universities, and the Forest Service (Powers and others 1996). The collaboration extended the LTSP program's reach to include industrial forests. Known as MPEQ for Monitoring Productivity and Environmental Quality in Southern Pine Plantations (MPEQ), the cooperative effort was organized and led by Allan Tiarks and Mason C. Carter, Professor at Louisiana State University, School of Forestry, Wildlife and Fisheries.

Another program like LTSP and MPEQ is the Center for International Forestry Research (CIFOR) studies, which established standardized experiments to study plantation productivity and sustainability on degraded soils in the tropics. Tiarks, the Forest Service representative in CIFOR's efforts, remained an active participant in CIFOR as an emeritus scientist after his retirement from Forest Service Research. The CIFOR studies tested management practices that not only prevent further degradation of the soil but also improve the long-term productivity of the site. Studies have been installed in seven tropical countries (Nambiar and others 2000).

When Tiarks retired in the late 1990s, D. Andrew (Andy) Scott was recruited to fill the LTSP soil scientist position. Scott demonstrated professional and leadership skills in assuming responsibility for the unit's program and became leader of the international LTSP program.

Aerial photo of the Long-term Soil Productivity installation on the Longleaf Tract. Note the 1-acre size of the treatment plots.

Stand management studies

When Philip Wakeley established the Palustris Experimental Forest and began evaluating nursery practices in 1935, he had foresight to install studies on long-term management practices for southern pines. These studies focused on planting spacing for longleaf and slash pine, prescribed fire, thinning, pruning, and stand stocking. So forward thinking was Wakeley that he used metric measurements to install his spacing study, reasoning that surely the United States would soon convert to the metric system.

The 1935 studies were adversely affected by wildfires in the 1940s, but the longleaf study survived to become one of the oldest research studies of the Southern Research Station, and today provides important information on the long-term management of longleaf pine.

Such studies led to another major area of research in the Research Center. This "growth and yield" research focused on how best to manage established pine plantations to maximize stand productivity. After World War II, many such studies were installed, both on the experimental forest and on lands of industrial cooperators in several States. In the 1980s, the "growth and yield" research involved more than 1,200 plots in dozens of studies, producing data sets that became a resource for developing computer-based stand projection models for land managers of southern pine plantation forests.

This photo was taken on the J.K. Johnson Tract of the Palustris Experimental Forest in April 1940. At the left rear is a longleaf plantation spacing study planted in 1934-35 that was controlled burned in January 1938. This study still provides significant information on the growth and yield of managed longleaf pine plantations. On the right rear is a slash pine spacing study planted at the same time that was destroyed when resources were lacking to protect the area from fire and animal damage.

FROM LEFT TO RIGHT: Station scientists T.R. Truax, George W. Tayer, Clarence L. Forsling, H.H. Muntz, John Curry, P.C. Wakeley, and C.L Bickford. The photo is by Station Director E.L. Demmon.

In 1955, the Louisiana Forestry Commission sponsored a German forester to come to the United States under a program that allowed entry of foreign citizens to provide technical expertise in areas where there were significant deficiencies in the United States. When Hans G. Enghardt and his wife arrived in Louisiana, he was assigned by State Forester James (Jim) Mixon to work at the Alexandria Research Center. Thus began a 30-year cooperative effort between the Research Center and the Louisiana Forestry Commission.

Enghardt conducted stand management research. He served as a State employee (in Louisiana) and collaborative scientist for 17 years. During this time, he gained U.S. citizenship and obtained a master's degree in forestry from Louisiana State University. He then returned to Germany to earn a Ph.D. and become a senior scientist for a German forestry organization.

The Louisiana Forestry Commission replaced Enghardt with Donald P. (Don) Feduccia, who remained in the position until budgetary considerations ended the long-term cooperative relationship in 1985. Feduccia brought excellent skills for stand management research and produced numerous significant publications that documented southern pine stand growth and yield research. After his return to the Forestry Commission, he served as Forest Management Chief for the State organization until his retirement in 2003.

The Southern Station hired a number of silviculturists and biometricians to supplement Louisiana's

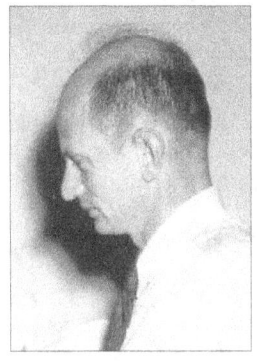

LEFT: Hans G. Enghardt, as a State of Louisiana employee, made significant contributions to stand management research.

RIGHT: Don Feduccia became forest management chief for the Louisiana Office of Forestry

scientists and conduct stand management research, including Richard L. Lohrey, V. Clark Baldwin, and Jeffery C.G. Goelz. Studies in plantation pine management earned the Alexandria Research Center a reputation as a leading research organization on managing southern pine forests. Results of some of these efforts are discussed in the following sections.

Planting spacing—Planting spacing recommendations vary depending on the characteristics of the species and the management goals of the landowner. Early tree planting recommendations for the United States were, however, influenced by European foresters (South 2003) who planted at a close spacing, 6- by 6-feet or closer, due to the slow growth of their species and the intensive

21

management of their stands. F.O. (Red) Bateman, ranger of the Great Southern Lumber Company, without much understanding of European practices, established the essentials of southern planting principles and techniques by 1922-23—dibble planting of bareroot nursery stock at a 6- by 8-foot spacing (Wakeley and Barnett 2011). The 6- by 8-foot spacing was economically and ecologically suitable for southern pines at that time and quickly became the standard spacing for planting southern pines.

However, Wakeley and other early researchers saw the need to evaluate a range of planting spacings. The experimental forest became the site of many of these studies. Wakeley's 1934-35 longleaf and slash pine plantations were the first spacing studies established on the forest. Both were adversely affected by neglect during World War II (Wakeley and Barnett 2011). However, when the study stands were at age 14, the survival of the slash pine study was sufficient for researchers to evaluate the spacings (Mann 1971). The number of trees per acre planted ranged from 4- by 4-feet, 6- by 6-feet, and 8- by 8-feet, to 10- by 10-feet spacing (about 2,700, 1,200, 680, and 435 seedlings per acre). A similar study with loblolly pine was installed in 1951-52. Planting spacings in this study were 6- by 6-feet, 8- by 8-feet, 9- by 9-feet, 10- by 10-feet, and 12- by 12-feet (Mann and Dell 1971).

The Louisiana Forestry Commission collaborated with the Southern Station in 1927-28 on a similar study of loblolly pine on another site nearby. The study

Close spacing at planting is best justified when there is a market for small stems, such as for fence posts or pulpwood.

investigated a range in spacing from 4- by 4-feet to 10- by 10-feet and provided needed information on effects of initial spacing on stand development (Feduccia and Mosier 1977).

In a more recent study in slash pine, seven spacing treatments between 4- by 4-feet to 14- by 14-feet showed that at age 15 tree heights in close spacings (4- by 4-feet to 6- by 6-feet) were shorter than in the three wider spacings (Ferguson and Baldwin 1995).

Selecting a spacing of 6- by 6-feet or less is normally impractical because of planting costs and dense stocking that retards diameter growth. For sawlog production, the 10- by 10-feet spacing may be best. It excels in diameter growth, but will have lower stem quality due to poor self-pruning. When markets for products from thinning are available, spacings of 6- by 6-feet or 8- by 8-feet, produce many trees of pole quality and thereby higher profits. These spacings also provide good cordwood volume growth.

Planting spacing recommendations vary greatly by landowner objectives and timber markets. Availability of valuable, fast-growing genetically improved planting stock favors a wide spacing to maximize returns. Many such stands are now commercially pruned. Within typical planting spacings, however, thinning regimes may affect the nature of timber quality more than does initial spacing (Baldwin and others 2000).

Precommerical thinning—Maintaining low stand densities can accelerate diameter growth, reduce rotations, shorten time to first thinning, and lessen potential fire mortality. High levels of stocking may negate these positive effects and result in overabundant seed trees in natural regeneration and less than ideal environmental conditions when direct seeding. Several thousand seedlings per acre can result and present a problem for the land manager. Studies on the experimental forest were installed to address this situation.

Slash and loblolly stands were established by direct seeding with the intent of obtaining high stocking levels (Lohrey 1972, 1973). Both studies resulted in over 5,000 seedlings per acre. When the stands were 3 years old, pre-commercial thinning—consisting of both selective hand and mechanical treatments—were installed. When the stands were 11 years old, results from the treatments were evaluated.

Results from these and other studies indicate that all stands with 5,000 or more stems per acre should be pre-commercially thinned. Stands should be thinned when the stands are about 3 years old to minimize costs and prevent reduction in live crowns. Reducing stocking to

LEFT: An unthinned 11-year-old slash pine with initial stocking of over 5,000 stems per acre.

RIGHT: An 11-year-old slash pine thinned by hand to 750 stems per acre at age 3 years

500 to 750 stems per acre will obtain optimum diameter growth without reducing volume production. Thinning by cutting swaths mechanically is as effective as selecting individual stems to be cut. Removing swaths about 10-12 feet wide will provide access for protection and stand management. Rotary mowers or rolling drum choppers are suited for the work (Lohrey 1977, Mann and Lohrey 1974).

Thinning: Initiation, Level, and Frequency—
Thinning as a stand management treatment has been studied intensively on the Palustris Experimental Forest with dozens of studies installed specifically to evaluate short- and long-term growth responses. These studies have been established with major southern pine species, on varying site qualities, and with a wide array of stand ages. They have been measured repeatedly, and the resulting data bases have become excellent resources for developing stand growth projection models for loblolly, slash, and longleaf pine.

Timing—As a general rule, thinning of pine stands should begin when their basal areas exceed 110 square feet per acre and when average tree diameter at breast height (d.b.h.) ranges from 5 to 9 inches (Feduccia 1983). How many years this takes will depend on species, initial spacing, survival, and site quality.

Methods—There are two broad alternative thinning methods for pine plantations: selective and mechanical. Selective thinning encompasses numerous methods in which trees are selected for removal on the basis of individual characteristics, including their relation to neighboring trees (Feduccia 1983). Typically, about two thinnings are needed to get a plantation in condition for sawtimber production. In these thinnings, suppressed, damaged, diseased, and rough stems are removed, and trees are taken to give the residuals adequate growing space. Any additional thinnings will remove some quality trees and improve economic returns.

LONG-TERM GROWTH AND YIELD STUDIES

Study and Species	Site Quality		
	Poor	Medium	Good
	Site Index 75-	Site Index 75-90	Site Index 90+
Density-growth relationships after commercial thinning			
Planted Stands			
Loblolly	0	X	X
Longleaf	X	X	X
Slash	X	X	X
Natural Stands			
Loblolly	0	0	0
Longleaf	X	X	X
Density-growth relationships after precommerical thinning in seeded stands			
Loblolly	X	X	X
Longleaf	X	X	0
Slash	X	X	x
Spacing-growth relationships in planted stands			
Loblolly	X	X	X
Longleaf	X	X	X
Slash	X	X	X
Spacing-growth relationships in row-seeded stands			
Loblolly	X	X	X
Longleaf	X	X	X
Slash	X	X	X

X – Established studies
0 – Future studies

This chart developed in the mid-1970s documents the scope of growth and yield studies established on the Palustris Experimental Forest and in the surrounding region.

In mechanical thinning, trees to be cut or retained are chosen on the basis of a predetermined spacing without regard to their position in the crown canopy. Row thinning is most commonly used in closely spaced plantations and leaves a higher percentage of smaller diameters, less vigorous trees in the lower crown classes (Baldwin and others 1989, Feduccia 1983). A modified row thinning treatment that incorporates some aspects of selective thinning can be accomplished by using equipment to do selective thinning in stands adjacent to the harvested row.

Intensity and frequency—The level or intensity of thinning refers to the amount of tree basal area left after a thinning and may be classified as heavy, medium, or light. Generally, heavy thinnings leave less than 75 square feet of basal area per acre, while moderate thinnings leave 75 to 90 square feet, and light thinnings left more than 90 square feet of basal area per acre (Feduccia 1983).

Regardless of thinning intensity, enough volume of wood products must be removed to make an economically operable cut. This varies by initial planting spacing, market conditions, geographical area, and considerations as a landowner. Close planting spacings require early thinning and a market for small sized products, such as pulpwood, and frequent subsequent thinnings. Wider planting spacings require fewer and lighter levels of thinning.

Heavy levels of thinning stimulate rapid diameter growth, but result in poorer stem form that lowers quality of potential wood products (Leduc and Zeide 1986, Lohrey 1983, 1985). Such thinning results in more and larger branches, crown length, and width; hence, weight and volume increase (Baldwin 1987, Baldwin and Feduccia 1987, Baldwin and others 2000).

Early growth and yield research had as a focus maximizing volume production from managed plantations. Planting spacings and thinning regimes to optimize early and frequent financial returns were used, and markets for products supported that approach. In more recent years, mechanization, shifts in market conditions, and labor availability have resulted in management practices that favor wider planting spacings and less need for frequent thinning.

Ideally, a thinning should be made each time the canopy closes, but this varies with the severity of the previous thinning and site productivity. However, the interval may also be governed by economic conditions. It could be as short as 3 years, but more likely at 5 to 10 years, the length increasing with age due to a reduction of diameter and basal area growth as the stand matures (Feduccia 1983).

Development of growth and yield computer simulation models (discussed in the following section) provides for a more sophisticated approach to establish thinning schedules. This approach allows the land manager to develop alternative thinning schedules and compare these alternatives using economic criteria (Dean and Baldwin 1993).

Stand yields and projections—Preparation of stand tables for the major southern pine species was an early and continuing research emphasis. These tables provided land managers with data to calculate product volumes, and they play an important role in growth and yield modeling (Cao and Baldwin 1999, Cao and others 1999, Leduc 2006). Such stand tables have been developed for unthinned slash pine plantations (Dell and others 1979, Lohrey 1987, Zarnoch and others 1991), loblolly pine (Baldwin 1987, Baldwin and Feduccia 1987, 1991, Feduccia and others 1979, Newbold and others 2001), shortleaf pine (Dell and others 1989), and longleaf pine (Baldwin and Polmer 1981, Leduc and Goelz 2009, Thomas and others 1995).

Stand table projection models provide for prediction of a future stand table based on the current stand table. Simple stand table projection models apply tree mortality information and diameter growth rates in adjusting stand tables (Cao and Baldwin 1999), and thus provide managers with predictions of product volumes and values to draft management decisions. Feduccia and others (1979) developed a computer program (USLYCOWP) for loblolly pine that would provide information on whether or not to thin, and if the

An example of row thinning. With modern equipment, such thinning will extend into the adjacent stands and the width of the removed material may need to be greater.

Loblolly pine plantation before initial thinning (age 25) planted at a 10- by 10-foot spacing. Note the poor self-pruning and the rough nature of the stems, but the good diameter growth.

Developing prediction systems for longleaf pine is difficult due to the uncertain delay in height growth initiation.

Longleaf pine seedlings in early height growth following herbicidal site preparation treatment to control herbaceous vegetation.

decision is to thin, how much and how often. Baldwin and Feduccia's (1987) COMPUTE_P-LOB model improved this earlier version to include unthinned stands older than 30 years old, as well as thinned stands with data through 45 years old. Ferguson and Baldwin (1987) provided a user's guide for COMPUTE_P-LOB that made it more user friendly.

Zarnoch and others (1991) developed a similar prediction system for slash pine that became known as COMPUTE_P-SLASH. The capability to predict fusiform rust infections was incorporated into this system (Nance and others 1985). An addition to the COMPUTE_P-LOB program was COMPUTE_MERCHLOB which is a growth and yield prediction system with a merchandising optimizer that allows a manager to incorporate product values into the system (Busby and others 1990).

Development of growth and yield prediction systems for longleaf pine has been difficult due to the uncertain age at which height growth begins. Most of the longleaf pine data bases represent a lengthy period when the seedlings were in the grass stage. Recent improvements in longleaf pine establishment present an opportunity to establish a realistic 1- to 3-year period for height initiation, and this provides an opportunity to develop height-diameter curves for longleaf pine plantations (Leduc and Goelz 2009).

In recent years, researchers have started using biological process models to predict forest productivity and to better understand growth process (Baldwin and Cao 1999). One approach to moving in this direction is to modify growth and yield prediction systems to incorporate biological processes. Clark Baldwin began a collaborative effort to link biological process to more traditional growth and yield models (Baldwin and others 1993, Baldwin and others 1998, Baldwin and others 2001).

Competition control with herbicides—Control of competing vegetation is an essential component of forest regeneration and afforestation. Vegetation adversely affecting pine establishment and growth can take several forms, including overstory of unmerchantable hardwoods, competing aborescent plants, and herbaceous plant development. Control of unmerchantable, low-quality hardwood overstories was a focus of early pine restoration efforts in the South, and herbicide technology developed (described in this book in the Control of Undesired Hardwoods section).

Fire for reducing competing vegetation has been a long-used silvicultural practice and is particularly important in longleaf pine restoration and management (see the Fire Research and Management section). However, development of some competing plant species cannot be easily controlled by fire, and in other instances, fire is not available as a management tool.

Use of herbicides to control aggressive grasses and forbs is a good option for releasing species like longleaf pine whose management depends on control of this type of vegetation. Use of herbicides is costly, and, if applied improperly, can injure desirable plants, animals (domestic and wildlife), and people, and can contaminate soil and water resources. Still, risks from using herbicides are frequently acceptable to obtain desired conditions in pine stands managed for multiple uses (Haywood 2009).

Selection of herbicides for appropriate species and sites varies by chemical availability, effectiveness, and desired method of application. Dave Haywood provides results of many studies where chemicals were used both for site preparation and post-planting competition control. For site preparation in advance of planting loblolly pine, these chemical applications included picloram pellets, liquid hexazinone, and a slurry of tebuthiuron powder (Haywood 1993). After planting, directed sprays of glyphosate, sulfometuron methyl, and hexazinone were applied to established loblolly pine seedlings (Haywood 1995, Haywood and Tiarks 1990, Haywood and others 2003). Reduced rates of glyphosate, oxyfluorfen and simazine were sprayed over the top of seedlings with little adverse effect (Haywood and Melder 1991).

Herbicides alone or in combination with fire or mechanical treatments to reduce herbaceous competition decrease how long longleaf pine seedlings remain in the grass stage, and promote sapling growth. Herbicides become a viable option for controlling competing vegetation in longleaf pine establishment when the use of fire is not available. Herbaceous vegetation can be controlled by spraying a low rate of hexazinone over the top of seedlings (Haywood 2000, 2005, 2007). Competing hardwoods can be controlled by chemical tricloplyr in directed sprays (Haywood 2009).

As a substitute for chemicals, commercial mulch mats and native pine needle litter are helpful in reducing vegetative competition, but neither is as effective as appropriate chemical applications (Haywood 2000).

Wood quality—Manipulating stands can change wood characteristics in plantation settings. Phil Wakeley planned stand treatments that would evaluate improving wood quality when he established his plantation studies in 1935. Other studies were installed many years later when the application of such treatments was more economically justifiable.

Pruning—A pruning treatment was planned in Wakeley's 1935 longleaf pine plantation study, and treatments were applied in 1950. Well-spaced trees were selected for testing pruning treatments: (1) pruning all trees per acre to a height of 17 feet; (2) pruning about 100 of the best trees per acre to 17 feet; and (3) pruning 100 of the best trees per acre to two-thirds of total height of the tree (Derr and Mann 1953).

Size of trees significantly influenced pruning costs. The cost for pruning a 4-inch tree at breast height was less

Harold J. Derr pruning longleaf pine in the plantation study established in 1934-35.

than half than that for an 8-inch tree. Pruning above the first log—17 feet—was expensive.

Pruning of longleaf pine appears most practical when trees average from 4 to 6 inches in d.b.h. Trees of this size will exceed 30 feet in total height. They can therefore be pruned to one log in a single operation, and they will retain over 40 percent of their live crown, which is enough for continued rapid diameter growth. Trees of this size will have a small core with knots and thus greater amounts of high grade lumber will be obtained.

At the time of this study, pruning was not an established practice. However, the study provided guidelines for establishing the commercial pruning operations now used by forest industry.

Sudden sawlog production—Derr's pruning results and data from other stand management studies indicated that quality sawlog trees could be grown in a much shorter time with intensive management. To demonstrate the effectiveness of stand treatments on improving lumber quality, James D. Burton installed what became known as the "sudden sawlog" study. At the time of installation, Burton was a staff member of the Crossett Research Center. When the Crossett Research Center closed in 1969, Burton was transferred to Gene Shoulders' newly created Intensive Culture Research Project in Pineville, LA. In 1982, the Intensive Culture Research Project was closed and integrated into the Forest Management Research Project.

Jim Burton was an advocate of using intensive management practices to improve wood quality.

Jim Burton standing in a 26-year-old sawtimber-pulpwood plot with a conventionally managed portion of the study in the background.

Burton evaluated four thinning regimes for loblolly pine plantations: (1) sawtimber only—stands thinned to 100 crop trees per acre at age 9, 76 stems per acre at age 19, and 64 at age 24; (2) sawtimber-pulpwood—stands thinned at ages 9, 12, and 15, leaving 100 trees per acre at age 15; and stands thinned to 80 trees per acre at age 19; (3) delayed sawtimber—stands thinned to 100 trees per acre at age 12, and 80 trees per acre at age 24; (4) control—stands thinned from below to 85 square feet basal area per acre at age 12 and every 3 years thereafter.

Crop trees were pruned to 50 percent of total height when thinning commenced and every 3 years thereafter until clear length of the stem averaged 33 feet when the stands were 24 years old. When the stands were 19 years old and thereafter, the understory was mowed every 2 years. Heavy thinning, pruning, and mowing gave the intensively managed stands an open park-like appearance.

Clearly, pine stands on good sites can be deliberately tailored for early harvests of sawlogs if the landowner so desires (Burton and Shoulders 1974). But, if landowners want maximum fiber yields at any age, greater returns from intermediate harvests, and narrow-ringed wood, they should choose conventional thinning. This treatment yielded 35 to 66 percent more merchantable cubic volume through 27 years than the intensive treatments. In 45-year-old stands, sawtimber volumes among the treatments were not significantly different (Baldwin and others 1998).

Landowners who want to grow sawtimber quickly should try one of the more intensive treatments tested in this study. Loblolly pine sawtimber with a mean d.b.h. of 15 inches was produced in 27 years through heavy thinning, understory control, and green pruning of limbs (Burton 1982).

Wood specific gravity of harvested 27-year-old trees was unaffected by treatment and was approximately equal to the local average for loblolly pine. These results demonstrate that high quality wood products can be produced when attention focuses on intensive stand management.

Woodpecker utility pole problems—Not just a wood quality issue, woodpecker use of wooden utility poles for nesting and roosting has long been a problem for utility companies. The problem is particularly significant when power lines run through swamps, river bottoms, and pecan groves, where red-headed (*Melanerpes erythrocephalus*) and pileated (*Dryocopus pileatus*) woodpeckers—the most destructive species in the South—are numerous.

Pileated woodpeckers cause significant damage to creosote-treated utility poles.

Bob Rumsey became a professor of wildlife biology at McNeese State University after leaving the Southern Research Station.

For some companies, damage from woodpeckers is as costly as lightning, wind, and ice. The traditional method for protecting poles placed in these locations is to wrap the utility pole in heavy-gage wire mesh. In the mid-1960s, five utility companies—Arkansas Power and Light, Central Louisiana Electric, Gulf States Utilities, Louisiana Power and Light, and Southwestern Electric Power—joined with Weyerhaeuser Company to fund a 5-year research project at the Alexandria Research Center to find a more effective and economical means of pole protection. Robert L. (Bob) Rumsey, a wildlife biologist, was hired by the Forest Management Project to conduct the research.

Woodpeckers evacuate holes of many sizes. The largest holes—cavities extending from 8 to 24 inches downward from an oval entrance that is 3 to 4 inches in diameter—are made by pileateds for nesting and roosting (Rumsey 1968). Ordinarily, a thin shell of wood is left around the cavity. The red-headed woodpecker makes the same shape nest but usually smaller. Other woodpecker species make smaller, less destructive holes.

Poles afford woodpeckers a broad, open view helpful in establishing and protecting territories. Birds are prone to excavate in the vicinity of burst checks in the pole. The most severe damage consists of nest and roost cavities; probe holes are much more numerous but are smaller and less weakening (Rumsey 1970).

Whether cavities are important entry points for decay is uncertain. Pileated and red-headed woodpeckers were attracted to white pine (*Pinus strobus*) tree sections attached to poles, but damage to poles with decoy sections still exceeded an acceptable level. Chemical repellents were unsuccessful, and a review of the morphology and physiology of woodpeckers fails to reveal a notable target in their sensory mechanisms.

There is no cheap, easy way to prevent woodpecker damage to wooden poles. Coatings or wraps offer some promise of protecting poles by making the surface too hard for the birds' talons to penetrate or too smooth to afford a perch. Such treatments, however, also make the poles difficult to climb by utility workers. Hardware cloth, although expensive, will continue to be used because its long-term effectiveness has been demonstrated.

Physiological Research
Although tree and seed physiology have been components of research in the experimental forest for decades, an emphasis on the physiological basis of seedling culture and silvicultural practices was initiated in the 1980s. The research sought an understanding of how seedlings, trees, and stands respond to manipulation, silvicultural practices, and environmental conditions. Information was developed on how to manage forest stands to compensate for shifting climatic patterns resulting from global warming. In addition, researchers focused on physiological effects of prescribed burning on long-term stand growth.

Seedling studies—Many nursery studies might fall under the category of physiological research, but two significant efforts associated with the experimental forest are based on physiology: The Reforestation Improvement Program and root zone studies.

Reforestation improvement program—The Reforestation Improvement Program was an effort to improve the quality of bareroot seedlings grown in Forest Service nurseries and to improve, and make more consistent, reforestation success (Owston and others 1990b). In 1986, the program teamed Forest Service research scientists with managers of all 10 current Forest Service nurseries. The researchers hoped to make reforestation more predictable and successful by (1) standardizing data collection and analyses, (2) improving knowledge of seedling biology through testing and observation, (3) reducing production costs and increasing the consistency of producing high-quality stock, and (4) enhancing knowledge of nursery environments and seedling physiology.

The researchers used two seed sources of major regional species, sown for 3 consecutive years. They applied an array of cultural treatments in the nursery, and monitored environmental conditions via automated weather stations in the nurseries and at field sites where outplantings were made. The weather stations recorded above-and belowground conditions on a continuing basis. The Palustris Experimental Forest was used for the field trials of loblolly, shortleaf, and slash pine seedlings were grown at the W.W. Ashe Nursery in Mississippi.

Weather stations were installed at all nurseries and field sites.

In addition to standard seed and seedling measurements, researchers in the nursery made detailed observations of seedling color and bud activity. As lifting time approached, researchers periodically measured root activity and plant moisture stress, and at lifting time, they assessed seedling size, color, mineral nutrient status, carbohydrate reserves, root-growth capacity, cold hardiness, and resistance to moisture stress.

John Brissette and Jim Barnett led the effort in the South with W.W. Ashe nursery manager, Charles (Chuck) Gramling. The mensurational and physiological measurements of seedlings were related to environmental conditions in the nursery and field. Of the physiological evaluations, root growth capacity was found the best comprehensive measure of seedling quality. Seedbed density, lifting date, and storage duration were found to affect root growth capacity and field survival of longleaf and shortleaf pine seedlings (Barnett 1991, Brissette and Barnett 1993).

Reforestation Improvement Program researchers also investigated the minimum temperature tolerated by container-grown longleaf pine roots and how to protect the roots from damaging cold. Roots of container seedlings held in outdoor nurseries in the fall and winter can be severely damaged by low temperatures. The freeze-induced electrolyte test was used to evaluate the cold hardiness of container longleaf pine seedlings. Results indicated that seedling roots should not be exposed to temperatures below 25 °F. A few degrees lower were lethal to roots (Sword and others 1999, Tinus and others 1999).

Results of the physiological studies with southern pine seedlings indicate that species and sources within species may differ dramatically in optimum lifting date. Ability to produce new roots is responsive to chilling hours, as is the ability of seedlings to maintain physiological vigor while in cold storage (Brissette

Root growth capacity misting chambers were developed to determine speed and length of new root development.

and others 1988). The Reforestation Improvement Program resulted in a better understanding of seedling physiology and how to improve seedling quality (Owsten and others 1990b).

Root zone studies—The second physiological effort evaluates root system growth and water transport of southern pine species after planting in different root-zone environments. This information is needed to guide decisions regarding when to plant and what species to plant. Researchers evaluated seedling root growth and water transport of three sources each of shortleaf, loblolly, and longleaf pine seedlings over 28 days in a seedling growth system that simulated planting environments (Brissette and others 1994).

Researchers developed the seedling growth system in a greenhouse where soil temperatures in the system could be kept at 55 °F, 65 °F, and 75 °F using water baths. Water availability was controlled by the distance root systems were suspended above water in a column; there was a well-watered control and two levels of water stress. After 28 days, plant moisture stress and root growth capacity were determined (Brissette and Chambers 1992).

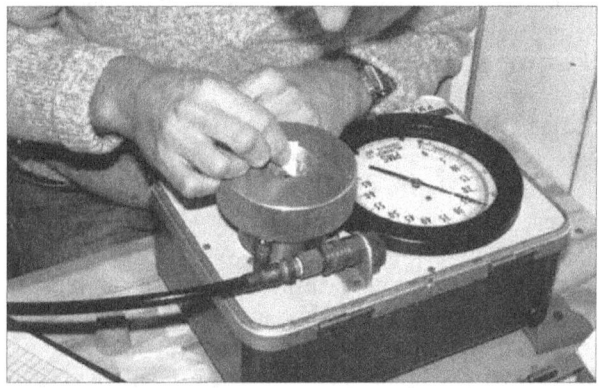

TOP: A plant moisture stress chamber for evaluating levels of stress in pine seedlings.

BOTTOM: Seedling growth system where control of different levels of root temperatures and moisture stress can be maintained.

Across species, an increase in root-zone temperature alleviated limitations to root growth caused by water stress. At the coldest temperature, longleaf pine maintained water transport greater than for shortleaf and loblolly pine. Without water limitation, root growth and water movement in longleaf pine was poorer than in the other species. As stress developed, longleaf pine responded more positively than shortleaf or loblolly pine. Therefore, there are significant differences among species in ability to function in stressful environments (Sword Sayer and others 2005).

In related research, scientists imposed water stress in sand beds developed in a greenhouse environment. Such stress beds provide excellent conditions for inducing water stress (Chambers and others 1988). With these beds, Reforestation Improvement Program scientists could evaluate the effects of J- or L-root deformity resulting from planting techniques on seedling survival. From their results, the researchers determined that depth of the root system upon planting was more important than curvature of the root system (Brissette and Barnett 1989).

Silvicultural practices—In 1988, research was undertaken in a 7-year-old loblolly pine plantation where unusual uniformity of tree growth had resulted from an earlier failed study (Barnett and Krugman 1989). The new researchers established 12 treatment plots with 13 rows of 13 trees each. In these plots, researchers imposed replicated fertilization and thinning treatments (Haywood 1994), evaluated treatments of throughfall exclusion of rainfall (Tang and others 2004b), and monitored environmental conditions both in the crown and soil.

Dan Andries and Mary Anne Sword Sayer at the tower site.

Jamie Tang conducting physiological evaluations of foliage on tower-supported walkways in tree crowns.

Mary Anne Sword Sayer determining root growth by using a mini-rhizotron system.

A tower system was developed to provide walkway access to two levels in crowns within the plots. Rhizotrons (soil pits with a Plexiglass® covered face) were used to measure root function. Sensors were installed at various levels to monitor physiological and environmental conditions in both crown and root systems using automated equipment (Sword and others 1998). One of the few studies where physiological data have been obtained from replicated stand measurements (most were done with only a few trees), the study became the basis for evaluating effects of treatment on both crown and root growth and development and their relationship to tree and stand physiology.

Mary Ann Sword was recruited to lead this research for the forest management staff. Collaborative research efforts were established with Jim L. Chambers of Louisiana State University's School of Forestry, Wildlife, and Fisheries, commencing a long-term cooperative research program that involved several graduate students, including doctoral research of Dennis A. Gravatt, Shufang Yu, and Zehenmin (Jamie) Tang.

The work of these collaborating scientists produced much published research on interactions among silvicultural manipulation, environmental conditions, and resulting physiological processes.

The published work offered a number of findings. Researchers reported that physiological and morphological characteristics of pine foliage were associated with differences in stand growth influenced by environmental changes and cultural treatments. Silvicultural manipulation causes microclimate changes within the crowns of large trees, but needle physiology adjusts to these within-crown environmental conditions (Tang and others 1999a). As light levels and crown exposure increase from thinning, photosynthesis activity increases in the lower portion of the crown (Tang and others 2003, 2004a). Thinning, fertilization, and crown position regulates annual leaf area production of current-year shoots largely by expanding the first flush shoots early in the growing season (Tang and others 1999b). Fertilization has little effect on foliage physiology, but it stimulates foliage production and thus improves growth (Tang and others 2003, Yu and others 2003). However, extended moisture stress reduces the potential of fertilization to stimulate growth (Sword-Sayer and Tang 2004, Tang 2004b).

Researchers also reported that root systems have limited ability to adjust to changing environmental conditions, but that the function of root systems is closely related to physiological processes in the crown (Sword Sayer and others 2004). For example, elevated root growth resulting from stand thinning is likely caused by an increase in the amount of photosynthate translocated from the crown (Sword and others 1998).

In addition, silvicultural treatments such as thinning and fertilization are effective through their influence on stand environment and resource variables and may be used to buffer possible negative effects, or enhance potential positive effects, of global climate change on southern pine forests (Sword and others 1998).

Fire effects—Land managers have limited their use of prescribed burning in managing most southern pine ecosystems, but fire remains an important silvicultural tool in the management of longleaf pine. Data have shown that repeated use of intense fire may adversely affect stand growth and development (Boyer 1987, Haywood 2009). To understand this phenomenon, studies were imposed in longleaf pine stands to determine effects of prescribed burning at various fire intensities and stand ages.

Scientists working in this research area found that severe crown scorch reduced longleaf pine diameter growth by 22 percent during five growing seasons after prescribed burning, and reduced root sucrose and starch concentrations, total and live fine root-mass density, and initiation of secondary root development (Haywood and others 2004). They also found that, even in moderate fires, root growth is less in plots burned in July than in those burned in March or May (Sword Sayer and Haywood 2006). These studies and others indicate that prescribed burning influences root growth by affecting mineral nutrition and root carbohydrate metabolism (Kuehler and others 2004).

Robert S. Campbell, an early range scientist, was a leader in establishing the American Society of Range Management.

Free-ranging hogs were a major cause of longleaf pine regeneration failures. Longleaf root systems are a choice source of nutrients in winter months.

In a study evaluating seasonal responses, a May treatment resulted in lower root starch concentrations but higher root glucose and potassium levels than in non-burned plots. Annual groundline diameter growth of saplings was increased, suggesting that fire shifts root carbohydrate and foliar potassium concentration in longleaf saplings to restore leaf area (Kuehler and others 2006). Starch reserves are high in May, and therefore May is a time to burn with little loss of tree growth. Starch reserves are lower in March and July and relate to poorer response from burning.

Range Management and Agroforestry

After the era of great lumbering ended, grazing livestock on forest range became a logical occupation for many residents of the piney woods. The upland soils were too poor for row-crop farming, but native forage was abundant and free (Cassady and Shepherd 1949). This situation existed across several million acres where forests had not recovered adequately after their harvest.

In 1944-45, Robert S. Campbell of the Southern Station in New Orleans conducted surveys of the grazing situation in Louisiana forest ranges and identified severe problems that needed study and correction.

Researchers found that meat production per animal was extremely low, as result of a combination of factors: deficiencies in native forage during fall and winter that were not compensated for by adequate supplemental feeding; poor-quality livestock; inadequate control of diseases and insects; and general lack of good management that went with free, unfenced forest range (Cassady and Mann 1954).

Grazing of livestock on forest ranges frequently prevented successful pine reproduction and growth. In addition to damage from animals, pine seedlings were destroyed by fires set by livestock owners to eliminate old grass and otherwise improve early grazing in spring. Livestock destroy pine reproduction directly by rooting, browsing, and trampling. Hogs, for example, relish longleaf pine seed and root up small pines to eat the fleshy part of the roots, which are nutritious.

With the establishment of the Alexandria Research Center in 1946, early surveys were used to initiate forest range grazing research in three closely related projects: management of livestock, management of forage, and improvement of forage (Cassady and Mann 1954).

During the 40 years of range-related research on the Longleaf Tract, emphases evolved from fairly straightforward tree/cattle relationships to multi-resource oriented research dealing with livestock,

Cattle sometimes push saplings over to browse on fresh shoots.

Poor quality range cattle were gathered for auction. Called scrub cattle, these cattle had limited commercial value.

wildlife, timber, fire, and watershed interrelationships. These changes resulted from improvements in range management practices, decline in traditional forest range programs, and development of more environmental programs with an agroforestry focus.

Livestock damage to plantations

Wild, free-ranging hogs can destroy longleaf pine plantations that are not fenced or otherwise protected for the first few years. In the 1940s, hogs were a source of meat for home use or ready cash. When there were no restrictions on free-ranging hogs, hogs were a major cause of longleaf pine reforestation failures. An adult hog can root up and kill seedlings at the rate of 5 or 6 per minute, and can destroy a whole acre of seedlings in a day or two (Cassady and Mann 1954). Longleaf pine seedlings are especially vulnerable because they have a large succulent root system and may remain in the grass stage for several years. "Hogs or logs" became a dilemma facing foresters, and was the title of a number of popular publications aimed at educating the public on the seriousness of the hog problem (Hopkins 1948).

Hogs will root up slash and loblolly seedlings, but their preference is longleaf pine (Peevy and Mann 1952). Over time, "hog laws" were passed curtailing open grazing of forest range. Although feral hogs are not now generally raised by locals as a source of food or income, they are released on public lands to provide for sport hunting. Thus, feral hogs continue to be a problem in forest management. Cattle can also damage plantation establishment and development—mostly by trampling seedlings, although they sometimes browse on pine shoots. Other damage may result from rubbing on young saplings to obtain relief from insect pests.

Stock laws now generally prevent livestock damage in plantations, but some may occur from cattle that graze under forest-range situations. This damage can

be limited by appropriate forage management (Cassady and others 1955).

Forage nutrient/supplemental feeding relationships

An early focus in the range program was to improve livestock nutrient on forest land, especially during the winter months when forage is limited. Cattle not provided with supplemental feed were in poor condition and brought little financial return to the owner. To overcome this problem, an understanding of plants available for grazing and their nutritional value was needed.

Although a plant collection and identification program had been ongoing at the Stuart Nursery since the mid-1930s, chiefly to help nursery staff develop more effective weed management options, range scientists expanded this effort beyond nursery boundaries. The recruitment of botanist Harold E. Grelen in 1962 began an emphasis on plant collection, identification, and specimen protection. Grelen established a herbarium to house and protect the plant collections. The herbarium became a resource for both range and forest research work units, and is now a valuable collection to support Kisatchie National Forest's botanical programs. Grelen led this effort and trained other scientific and technical staff on identifying plants and protecting collected material.

With information on types of plants available for cattle grazing (Grelen and Duvall 1966), cooperative efforts began with Louisiana State University to analyze plants to determine their nutritional value. This research identified nutritional deficiencies in forage available to range stock, and led to recommendations for supplemental feeding that significantly improved livestock quality (Pearson and others 1982).

Providing supplemental feed became a widely accepted practice for cattlemen interested in improving the

Harold E. Grelen led the range unit's botanical program until his retirement in 1986.

TOP: *Range cattle are provided supplemental feed during the winter months to maintain weight and health.*

BOTTOM: *An aggressive burning program controls hardwood understory vegetation and provides good forage for grazing of livestock.*

Captive deer were used to determine diets on prescribed burned and grazed forest ranges. Alton Martin, Jr., range technician in the background, records species of plants browsed. Martin received the U.S. Department of Agriculture Distinguished Service Award in 1990 for his work in plant identification.

economic returns from their cattle operations on southern pine-bluestem land (Grelen and Pearson 1977, Pearson and Rollins 1987, Pearson and Whitaker 1972).

Soil and water effects

Concentrations of cattle in areas such as paddocks result in soil compaction and impaired water infiltration. Grazing studies on the Longleaf Tract provided an opportunity to evaluate effects on soil compaction and water infiltration under forest-range conditions. After 10 years of varying grazing intensities (none, moderate, and heavy) and three prescribed burning treatments (no burn, controlled burn, and wildfire), evaluations indicated that heavy grazing compacted soils sufficiently to restrict water movement into and through the profile especially during intense rainstorms (Linnartz and others 1966). In addition to impaired infiltration, the heavy grazing treatment markedly reduced native grasses and increased a higher proportion of less desirable carpet grass (*Axonopus fissifolius*) (Duvall and Linnartz 1967). In this study, fire had little long-term effect.

In another study of grazing and silvicultural practices, surface cover and bulk density were influenced mostly by silvicultural treatments. Grazing treatments affected grass cover and biomass. However, under the prevailing climatic, soil, and vegetative conditions of the study area, the impacts of applied silvicultural and grazing practices on infiltration and runoff water quality did not present a problem to site management or productivity (Wood and others 1989).

Prescribed burning

Prescribed fire plays an integral role in forest-range management. Burning areas on a 3-year rotation controls the development of understory hardwood competition, reduces pine needle litter build up, increases herbage yield and nutrient composition, and favors regeneration of longleaf pine by either natural or artificial techniques.

Early in the range research program, effects of frequent use of prescribed burns were evaluated as a way to improve forage production and quality. Duvall and

Whitaker (1964) and Grelen and Epps (1967) found that burning different portions of a range in winter, spring, or summer provided quality protein in herbage for a much longer period than winter burning alone. They also found that removal of pine needle litter was a major factor in the positive response from frequent burning.

Grelen's (1975, 1983) research also established that prescribed burning in May not only was more effective in controlling woody vegetation than in dormant winter months, but also increased survival and growth of longleaf pine seedlings. This research led many organizations to begin conducting spring burns, which have proven more effective in reducing hardwood competition and stimulating early height growth of longleaf pine seedlings. Spring burning is not only good for improving forage for livestock, but it also has become an important component of longleaf pine management (see Fire Research and Management, Long-term Fire Studies section).

Cattle/deer diet interactions

Aggressive prescribed burning to enhance forage availability and quality are part of southern range management, but wildlife specialists began looking at how these practices might reduce deer habitat. Ronald E. (Ron) Thill, of the range research work unit, began studying the effects of prescribed burning and grazing programs on the extent of seasonal diet overlap between deer and cattle on areas subjected to moderate yearlong cattle grazing.

To carry out this research, young captive deer were tamed and harnessed and then allowed to feed in the treatment areas. Food preferences of deer, while on leash, were documented. Studies showed that wild deer and tame deer both preferred the same plants (Thill 1984).

Researchers found that deer diets were dominated yearlong by a mixture of browse and herbage, and that cattle consumed mostly grasses in the spring and summer and 69 and 40 percent browse and herbage, respectively, during the fall and winter (Thill 1989). Diets of both animals were diverse and generally resulted from sharing small amounts of many plant taxa. Types of plants eaten by deer were more affected by burning than grazing, but deer selected more herbage and less browse on grazed than on ungrazed sites (Thill 1986).

Researchers also learned that late-spring through early-fall grazing should have little negative impact on deer forage availability. During this period, cattle diets consisted primarily of grasses, while deer consumed mostly browse and herbage. Diet overlap was highest from fall through early spring as both types of animals sought diets from a limited supply of evergreen browse and herbaceous winter forbs. Consequently, even

moderate cattle stocking during this period could reduce available deer forage significantly (Thill 1989). On more open sites, however, forage is sufficiently abundant enough to meet needs of both cattle and deer (Thill and others 1987).

Tree/forage/cattle management

Grazing of forest land in the South began soon after harvest of old-growth forests. The use of forest land for open-range livestock production was characterized by complete lack of management. As reforestation efforts began, landowners realized that if a combination forest and range management was to be successful, modifying practices that optimized each would be needed.

Researchers found that intensity and duration of grazing have significant effects on availability and quality of herbage and browse. Total herbage yields were not appreciably changed by light yearlong cattle grazing which removed 30 to 60 percent of the annual growth (Pearson and Whitaker 1973). However, moderate and heavy grazing reduced desirable bluestem frequency and increased undesirable carpet grass understory. They also learned that, although heavy grazing adversely affected planted and seeded slash pine, neither light nor moderate grazing by cattle affected establishment and survival of trees younger than 5 years old (Pearson and others 1971). When the trees were measured at 18 years old, researchers found that heavy grazing reduced survival of trees, but that light to moderate grazing was compatible with establishment and growth of slash pine (Grelen and others 1985). From these results, the researchers concluded that some regulation of levels of grazing was necessary to accommodate successful plantation establishment.

Researchers found that, as plantations continued to age and basal area increased, herbage production declined. Crown closure reached levels sufficient to reduce forage at age 10 years for slash pine and 17 years for longleaf

LEFT: *Ron Thill transferred to Nacogdoches, TX, and became project leader of a wildlife research work unit.*

RIGHT: *Gale L. Wolters, forest-range ecologist, researched overstory-understory plant relationships on the Longleaf Tract until he was transferred to the Pacific Southwest Research Station.*

A productive forest range requires low stand densities that allow light to the forest floor and light to medium levels of cattle stocking that maintain plant quality and quantity.

Developing training procedures for adding range information into the forest survey.

pine (Wolters 1982). Not only was amount of herbage reduced, but also the composition was affected as pine basal area increased. Amounts of bluestem grasses decreased, and forbs increased as light levels to the ground floor declined (Byrd and others 1984). Loblolly-shortleaf pine-hardwood stands had similar effects, except that shrubs and hardwood crown cover affected herbage production of quality (Wolters and others 1982). Uniola grasses were the principal forage species under high density stands while bluestems were the major forage component in clearings.

Early use of prescribed burning in slash pine plantations did not prevent herbage yields from dropping sharply as the overstory developed (Grelen 1976). Early burning prevented most hardwoods and shrubs from reaching size uncontrollable by fire, kept browse accessible to cattle and deer, and prevented pine litter from eliminating herbaceous plants from the understory. It had no effect on pine survival and growth.

As pine stands reach a size for initial thinning, forage production declines significantly. Thinning levels needed to maintain adequate forage production for cattle grazing are considerably lower than for operational forestry practices. Lundgren and others (1983) base their range economic assessments on maintaining a pine stand residual basal area of about 70 square feet—compared with about 85 square feet per acre for forestry operations. Under these range conditions, light levels are adequate to allow a forage understory that can support a moderate number of cattle.

A multi-resource program in livestock, trees, and wildlife must bring together information and specialists who have the capability to combine a number of

interacting resources. This requires ingenuity, commitment, and dedication. To be effective, a broad ecological approach must be maintained.

Forest survey
The Forest Service has responsibility for conducting nationwide forest surveys for the collection and analysis of information from forest and forest-related lands. The surveys are traditionally conducted to provide data on timber and wood products. In 1973, inventory and analysis of range resources was added to the survey process in the South (Sternitzke and Pearson 1974). Methodologies and training procedures were developed and tested, and survey crews were trained on the Longleaf Tract prior to field application (Pearson and Sternitzke 1974).

Economics
Pearson (1982) and his colleagues (Lundgren and others 1983, 1984) conducted thorough analyses of the economics of forest-range grazing when timber and livestock prices were stable. To evaluate efficiency in forest grazing, they analyzed annual economic return assuming a 40-year timber rotation that included two thinnings (years 15 and 27) with one of three levels of cattle stocking allowed to graze pastures for varying lengths of time. They found that rotating cattle through the timberland was more economical than continuous grazing, which yielded the lowest rate of return (4.5 percent). The highest cattle stocking combined with the shortest grazing duration yielded the greatest rate of return (8.2 percent).

The range management research unit closed 10 years after these analyses because of shifts in research priorities and budgetary limitations. However, a basic

Henry A. Pearson receiving the W.R. Chapline Research Award from the Society of Range Management.

A challenge in creating and maintaining agroforestry programs is finding an economical and biological balance in managing multiple resources.

problem was the decline in numbers of livestock managers interested in forest range grazing due to curtailment of prescribed burning and conversion of range lands to other uses (Grelen 1978). Permits for grazing on Federal land also became more expensive and difficult to obtain. Also, second-generation families lost interest in forest-range grazing, and higher levels of ecological understanding were needed to profitably graze in forested situations.

In the 1980s, Pearson began broadening the perspective of the traditional forest-range grazing research program to encompass agroforestry. To evaluate alternatives that enhance farm flexibility by use of multiple commodities, researchers from the U.S. Department of Agriculture and the New Zealand Forest Research Institute joined forces in developing the United States Agroforestry Estate Model (USAEM). USAEM was adapted from the New Zealand Agroforestry Estate Model that incorporates tree growth and yield models, farm crop data, and livestock forage production (Pearson and others 1995).

In developing the USAEM model, researchers demonstrated that agroforestry could be profitable and appropriate for family farms using land in the mid-South. Shifts in research priorities and funding curtailed full development and application of the model.

Agroforestry

Agroforestry integrates the interactive benefits of trees, crops, and livestock. It combines forestry and agricultural technologies to create more diverse, productive, profitable, and sustainable land-use systems. Under this definition, grazing forested land could be considered a form of agroforestry.

In the 1980s, Project Leader Henry A. Pearson led an effort to enhance the Palustris Experimental Forest's range program by seeding forest range with subterranean clover. This clover can reseed naturally and will tolerate prescribed fire and heavy grazing. When combining pines and cattle on pasture, grazing is often delayed for several years until trees are large enough to resist browse damage. Subterranean clover treatments were imposed to provide additional forage during this early pine seedling development stage (Pearson and others 1990a). Results indicated that clover improved forage, but that electric fencing placed directly over the planted rows of trees was necessary to avoid serious seedling injury from trampling.

Two other agroforestry approaches were evaluated: combining Christmas tree production with grazing (Pearson and others 1990b); and combining timber production, grazing, and pine straw harvest for the landscape industry (Haywood and others 1995). Longleaf is the preferred species for harvesting because its long needle length facilitates baling and handling.

Whit Whitaker, range technician, lived and worked on the Longleaf Tract for many years. For his excellent technical support, he received the U.S. Department of Agriculture Superior Service Award.

37

Of agroforestry practices evaluated on the Palustris Experimental Forest, pine straw harvesting has shown the greatest potential for supplementing income to land owners. Pine straw is a renewable resource that is harvested primarily for landscaping mulch. Recently, its use in landscaping dramatically increased. Adding straw to timber and forage as products of management can increase profits substantially, and the income from straw may actually exceed that from timber itself (Haywood and others 1996).

In spite of immediate economic opportunities, scientists were concerned that repeated removal of the forest floor could adversely affect pine growth and yield. Therefore, a large study was installed on the Palustris Experimental Forest to determine how pine straw harvesting practices influenced longleaf pine productivity. Results showed that harvesting pine straw can increase soil bulk density, soil movement, potassium concentrations in the mineral soil, and water turbidity. Harvesting can also reduce water infiltration, pine tree growth, and fire hazard. Some of these problems can be reduced by proper management.

Researchers developed a recommended formula for compensating for nutrient losses from straw removal: periodic fertilization with 150-200 pounds of nitrogen per acre (Morris and others 1992) and 50 pounds of phosphorus per acre. They also recommended that landowners should avoid harvesting on soils with more than 10 percent slopes and stream-bottom areas, and rake straw carefully to prevent loss of mineral soil. The researchers concluded that, although negative effects may not be entirely reversed with several years of rest from harvesting, the economic value of carefully collected straw may outweigh the cost of damage.

Intensive Culture Research

Elements of intensive culture research had long been a part of Forest Management Research. But to enhance this phase of research, a separate research work unit was created in 1969 at the Alexandria Research Center. Eugene (Gene) Shoulders was named project leader of the Intensive Culture Research Work Unit and charged with maximizing productivity of southern pine plantations. The work included reassigning parts of the Crossett Research Center program (in Crossett, AR)—such as forest genetics, soils, and stand management—to the new unit. As well, components of the Pineville Forest Management Research Work Unit—such as site preparation, post-planting competition control, and irrigation—were assigned to Shoulder's unit. Although the research assignment was broad, soils and fertilization were the primary themes.

Gene Shoulders, long-term Forest Management Work Unit scientist, was reassigned to lead the new intensive culture project.

The Intensive Culture Research Work Project functioned independently from 1969 until 1982, when it returned to the fold of Forest Management Research. The following are significant research efforts from the work undertaken in this project related to the Palustris Experimental Forest.

Soils

In the West Gulf Coastal Plain, wet pine-growing soils are saturated for prolonged periods in winter but dry out in summer and may intermittently develop serious moisture deficits (Shoulders and McKee 1973). This situation is much different than for sites further east, where water may be over abundant for long periods in all seasons.

For 8-year-old slash pine, beds that raised the water table 18 inches or more above the water table during January and February were effective in promoting tree growth, whereas beds that raised the soil less than 18 inches resulted in one-third less aboveground biomass (5.4 tons oven-dried weight).

Bedding became the most popular and perhaps the only practical method of removing excess water from the rooting zone and improving soil aeration. Growth response to bedding varies significantly (Derr and Mann 1977, Mann and Derr 1970), largely because of differences in the amount of well-aerated soil bedding provides during the wet winter period (McKee and Shoulders 1970, 1974).

On the poorly drained silt-loam soils of west central Louisiana, effective beds are difficult to construct, and if not properly constructed, may reduce rather than enhance pine growth. The continuous nature of beds sometimes aggravates the situation by impeding drainage of water. Discontinuous beds were proposed to improve water flow, but they were difficult to build and resulted in site conditions that restricted logging and management operations (Haywood 1981). Numerous studies indicate that bedding on many sites yielded no long-term benefits and may actually result in lower productivity in the following rotation.

Discontinuous beds were proposed to allow better drainage of water, but building them was difficult and they resulted in site conditions that limited management operations.

Other site preparation treatments, such as disking, improve pine plantation success and early growth primarily by reducing competition from herbaceous vegetation (Tiarks and Haywood 1981).

Fertilization

Soils of the West Gulf Coastal Plain differ from those of the Southeast by having lower levels of phosphorus (Shoulders and McKee 1973). The soils are also low in nitrogen and potassium, and on many sites, waterlogging affects response to fertilizers (McKee and Shoulders 1974). A challenge for Gene Shoulders and his colleagues was to determine not only the nutrient needs of the soils but also how these are modified by waterlogged conditions, and when and how best to apply fertilizers under operational conditions.

Application of phosphorus and nitrogen to forest soils of the West Gulf Coastal Plain provides the most positive gains in growth. Studies have shown that application rates of 100 pounds of each per acre are effective (McKee 1973, Shoulders and McKee 1973, Shoulders and Tiarks 1980a).

Although fertilizer applications to newly planted pines can increase early growth, field observations indicate the effect of fertilizer is often negated by herbaceous plant competition because these plants respond faster than pines to added nutrients (Tiarks and Haywood 1981). Based on these observations, the researchers concluded that fertilization at planting or during early plantation establishment should be accompanied by competition control, and that once young stands achieve closed canopies, understory plant development is limited and effective fertilization can be obtained through broadcast applications by plane or ground equipment. The method has become a common practice for increasing tree growth and improving plantation profits.

Applying fertilizers in bands with ground equipment is effective once tree crowns begin to close.

Post-planting competition control

The need for post-planting competition control was demonstrated by a unique study (Tiarks and Haywood 1981). To determine the amount of control needed, fertilized and unfertilized rows of planted slash pine were hand-hoed in a wedge-shaped pattern. By using this technique, the amount of cultivation varied from none to complete.

After 4 years, fertilization or complete competition control were about equally effective in improving biomass production. When these treatments were combined, they interacted to increase biomass by 347 percent (Tiarks and Haywood 1981). Although complete control is necessary near seedlings to maximize early growth of the pines, some ground cover should remain to limit soil erosion.

Other studies installed in operational plantings confirm that a combination of weed control and fertilization is needed to maximize pine growth and development (Moehring 1966).

Irrigation

Research in the West Gulf Region indicated that early growth of pine plantations may be boosted if summer water deficits are alleviated by irrigation (Moehring 1964). Although irrigation was a treatment considered for use in maximizing growth of pine stands, researchers determined early that practical application of irrigation treatments was not feasible in most plantation environments. In a study on the Experimental Forest where the capability for irrigation was installed, seldom was the moisture deficit criteria met that required its application.

Insect and Disease Research

Research on insect and disease problems was a part of the timber management program of the Alexandria Research Center before Forest Service Research reorganized in 1964. Most problems related to insects and diseases were assigned to other research work units, but research on some pests continued as needed to conduct forest management research.

Early in planting studies, Texas leaf-cutting ants (*Atta texana*), also known as town ants, brown-spot needle blight, and fusiform rust (*Cronartium quercuum* f.sp. *fusiforme*) were pests that often limited plantation success. These pests became the focus of some research carried out on the Palustris Experimental Forest and surrounding forests.

Town ant biology and control

Town ants were a major hazard to pine seedlings in the uplands of central Louisiana and east Texas. The ants destroy young pines by stripping off needles and terminal buds or by cutting the radicle and cotyledon tissue from germinating seeds. They carry green plant material into underground chambers, where the plant material forms the fungal substrate that each colony cultures for food.

Ant colonies are identifiable by mounds of excavated soil clustered above the general region of the fungus chambers. A single mound usually signifies a new colony; old colonies may have 300 or more mounds distributed over one-quarter of an acre (Echols 1966). One colony is capable of destroying several acres of planted seedlings, and the economic impact in Louisiana was recognized as early as 1934, when large-scale planting projects were started.

Beginning in the early 1940s, destroying colonies by fumigating them with methyl bromide became the standard control treatment (Johnson 1944), and continued as such for 25 years. Due to significant

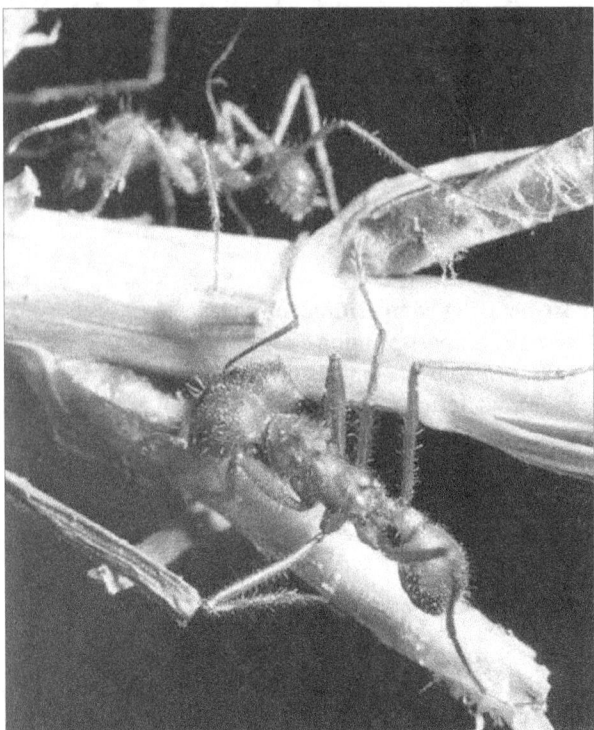

Town ants range from ¼ to ¾ inch long and are very efficient in cutting pine needles, terminal buds, and germinating seed tissue to supply their fungus gardens.

John C. Moser examines a town ant fungus garden chamber during the evacuation of a large ant colony.

damage to pine plantations from town ants and problems with the use of methyl bromide, entomologist John C. Moser was added to the staff of the Alexandria Research Center in 1959 to conduct additional research. Moser's approach was to understand the biology of the town ant. He reviewed the literature on similar species in South America and, with help from the forest industry, excavated a large colony for study. Three years later, he published a comprehensive article on the biology of town ants (Moser 1963).

With the reorganization of Forest Service Research in 1964, Moser was transferred to a newly created forest insect research unit in Pineville, LA. However, his passion for understanding the biology of town ants did not end. He continued to study the ants and their related insect species, even when the research was outside the unit's mission, and he became the international expert on leaf-cutting ants as well as the mites and other insects that coexist with the ants.

Forest Management Research recruited Hamp W. (Bill) Echols to develop a control treatment for this species that limits pine reforestation success (Shoulders 1960). Fortunately for Echols, Mirex® was being developed to control fire ants (*Solenopsis invicta*), which had become a serious pest across the South. Echols found that a formulation of Mirex® controlled town ants as well (Echols 1965, 1966).

As registration efforts for the town ant formulation of Mirex® continued, the U.S. Congress approved the aerial spraying of the fire ant formulation. Most rural areas in the South where fire ants were a problem were sprayed several times. Not only did the chemical greatly reduce populations of fire ants, but it also significantly reduced the number of town ant colonies. However, aerial spraying of the pesticide ended in 1977 due to environmental concerns. Not as aggressive as fire ants, which quickly recovered from the pesticide, town ants are only now recovering and filling their earlier niche in the forest landscape.

Brown-spot needle blight
Early in the initiation of a reforestation program for longleaf pine, brown-spot needle blight was a major problem. Described by Siggers (1932), it is a disease that affects seedlings both in the nursery and in the field. Lesions may develop on secondary needles at any time, but they most commonly appear in late summer. Typically they appear as straw-yellow bands that turn light brown with chestnut-brown margins on needles. Ascospores, disseminated by wind and rain splash, spread infections. Spore forms overwinter in dead and infected needle tissue. Thus, seedlings that are in the grass stage are subject to repeated infections that increase the seriousness of the disease.

Station scientist H.H. Muntz sprays longleaf pine seedlings in the Stuart Nursery with a Bordeaux® mixture to control brown-spot needle blight. Civilian Conservation Corps employees are providing technical support.

Infected seedlings in the nursery are seldom killed, but severe defoliation reduces vigor, which may result in poor survival and growth following outplanting. For decades, the common treatment in nurseries was spraying beds of longleaf pine seedlings with a Bordeaux® mixture (Wakeley 1954). More recently, it has been found that almost any fungicide will control the disease, and several are registered for use on brown-spot infections (Kais 1989).

Brown-spot infections have been a major factor delaying height growth of planted longleaf pine seedlings. Seedlings may remain in the grass stage up to 10 years when infections are severe. In this stage of low vigor, seedling mortality may occur. The simplest method of reducing the level of brown-spot infections in the field is to use prescribed fire. Prescribed burning every 2 or 3 years destroys the infected needles and thus kills the spores. Reinfestations will occur, but the seedlings have an opportunity for enough development to initiate height growth.

Researchers suggested that another control treatment is application of a root dip of 5-percent active ingredient benomyl-kaolin clay or similar fungicidal-clay mixture at lifting of seedlings in the nursery (Barnett and Kais 1987). Studies found that such treatment not only reduces brown-spot infestations in the field but also improves seedling survival by reducing pathogens that reduce seedling vigor during cold storage.

Brown-spot blight is much less a problem in longleaf pine reforestation today than a number of decades ago. The limited numbers of longleaf pine seedlings remaining in the grass stage has reduced the source of disease inoculum. With improved success in seedling establishment and faster height initiation resulting from better nursery and site preparation methods, opportunities for spore populations to build to damaging levels are limited.

A seed coat dropped from the seedling following germination may carry fungi that cause seedling mortality.

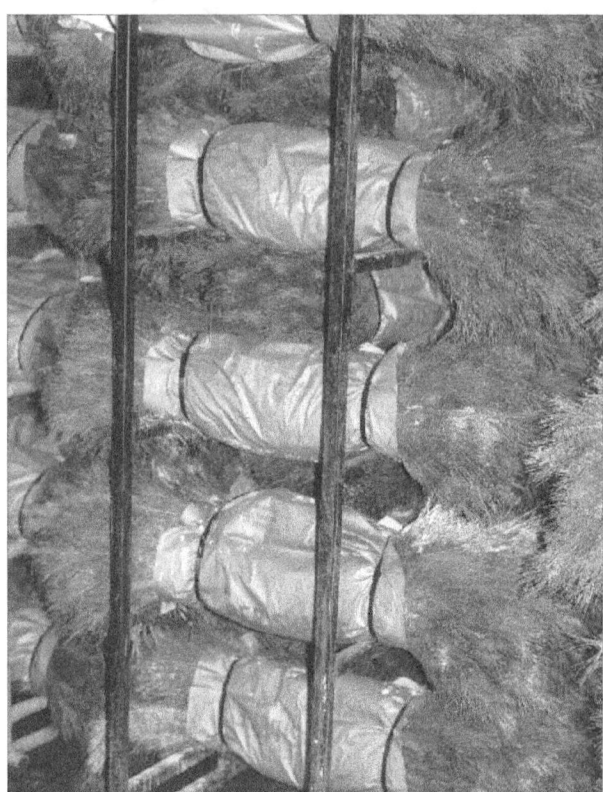

Pine seedlings with roots sprayed with a benomyl-clay slurry prior to being placed in cold storage.

Seed, seedling, and root storage pathogens

Longleaf pine seeds are large, have fibrous seed coats, and generally carry a host of microorganisms. On low vigor seeds, the fungi may be pathogenic and significantly reduce seed germination and infect newly germinated seedlings. Early studies showed that eliminating the fungi by hydrogen-peroxide sterilization significantly improved seed performance (Barnett 1976c).

Research also showed that fungicide benomyl (Benlate®)—applied to bareroot nursery stock by dipping root systems in fungicidal-clay slurries—controlled brown-spot needle disease and improved longleaf pine seedling survival (Barnett and Kais 1987). Based on the finding, further study found that benomyl and related fungicidal treatments were effective in improving both seed germination and seedling development (Barnett and others 1999).

Advances in container nursery technology led to evidence that seedlings were frequently infected from fungi on seed coats (released from germinating seeds) that fall into containers after germination. Without fungicidal treatment of seed coats, mortality of longleaf seedlings may occur frequently in the container nurseries (Barnett and McGilvray 2002b).

Fungicidal root dips for controlling brown-spot needle blight were so effective in improving bareroot

seedling survival that researchers hypothesized those microorganisms were reducing seedling vigor during cold storage of longleaf pine seedlings. Longleaf pine seedlings are difficult to store, a factor making reforestation of this species problematic. A number of field studies were installed to evaluate benomyl-clay slurry dips with varying periods of cold storage of longleaf, loblolly, and shortleaf pine seedlings. Results of these tests indicated that fungicide applications were positive when applied in many nurseries producing bareroot longleaf pine seedlings (Barnett and others 1988, Brissette and others 1996).

John P. Jones of Louisiana State University's Department of Plant Pathology and Crop Physiology began cooperative research to identify the pathogens associated with mortality of seeds and seedlings and determine if causes for the loss of vigor during seedling storage were disease related. He and his researchers learned that the benomyl-clay slurry root treatment was controlling fungi that were reducing performance of longleaf pine bareroot stock during cold storage. Jones and graduate student Xiaoan Sun then conducted a number of tests to identify causal microorganisms (Jones and others 1992, 1997).

Results indicated that both *Fusarium* and *Pythium* fungi were involved in the seed and root disease problems. One specific fungus (*Fusarium circinatum*)

Slash pine seedlings with stem swellings that indicate fusiform rust infections.

Scientist Harold J. Derr pointing to fusiform rust galls in sapling stems in a slash pine plantation.

was identified in the root disease problem (Jones and others 1999), but other species of *Fusarium* and *Pythium* was also involved in seed, seedling, and root problems. Sun and others (1993) identified a species of *Trichoderma* that might be developed as a biological control of the root storage pathogens. Fungicides that effectively controlled these diseases were identified, and Jones and others (2002) investigated nursery cultural practices that may limit the seriousness of these disease problems in the nursery.

Fusiform rust
Fusiform rust is the most damaging disease of southern pine plantations. It occurs in a broad band across the Southern States and is most prevalent in highly productive loblolly and slash pine plantations. Rust incidence has increased dramatically in the last 30 to 40 years, especially in intensively cultured stands. Fusiform rust galls have been tallied routinely along with other stand measurements in studies on the Palustris Experimental Forest, but in the early 1980s, infestations became severe enough to cause significant losses in stand productivity and even mortality.

Early attempts to control fusiform rust infections focused on culling seedlings with visible rust cankers during lifting at the nursery. Unfortunately, a study showed that many seedlings may have rust infections that only appear after outplanting (Czabator and

Enghardt 1959). A follow-up study demonstrated that pruning infected limbs of young slash pines in the field to reduce fusiform rust damage was neither effective nor economical (Enghardt and others 1969). Clearly, a chemical treatment was needed to protect seedlings from rust infections.

In the early 1980s, the systemic chemical triadimefon (Bayleton®) was found effective in controlling fusiform rust in pine seedling nurseries (Snow and others 1979) and was tested as a treatment to protect young outplanted stock. It showed good potential as a treatment for young slash pine plantings (Burton and Snow 1983).

A large study was installed on the Palustris Experimental Forest to evaluate the effect of fungicidal spraying on fusiform rust infections on slash pine subjected to a wide range of cultural regimes (Burton and others 1985). The eight treatments were (1) no fungicide, weed control, or fertilizer; (2) weeded; (3) weeded, applied inorganic fertilizer, and bedded before treatment; (4) weeded, bedded, and applied inorganic fertilizer in the sixth growing season (delayed fertilization); (5) applied fungicide but no weed control or fertilizer; (6) applied fungicide and weeded; (7) applied fungicide plus treatment 3; and (8) applied fungicide plus treatment 4.

Fungicides were applied five times annually. For the first 4 years, herbicides were used to obtain complete control of understory vegetation. Treatments were assessed 10 years after planting. Fungicide treatments resulted in higher survival, fewer trees with stem galls, fewer galls encircling the stem, and greater total volume per acre (Haywood and others 1994). Fertilization and weed control generally increased tree height, diameter, and corresponding volume production, but were associated with a greater incidence of fusiform rust, which normally occurs when unimproved slash pines are outplanted and intensively cultured.

The documentation of fusiform rust galls in Shoulder's "choice of species" study (see Site-species Relationships section), which had 113 installations across Louisiana and southern Mississippi, provided data to model relationships of fusiform rust incidence to survival and yield of unthinned slash and loblolly pine plantations (Nance and others 1985; Shoulders and Nance 1987). Shoulders and Nance's (1987) work indicated that loblolly pine was more resistant to fusiform rust infections than slash pine. The results were later verified by Walkinshaw and Barnett (1995). The research of Shoulders and his colleagues has provided the most complete understanding to date of the relationship of fusiform rust to species, cultural, and edaphic variables.

Fire Research and Management

Fire effects in southern pine forests have been studied since forestry research was initiated in the early 1920s. Prescribed burning was a component in plantation studies that Wakeley installed on the Palustris Experimental Forest in the winter of 1934 to 1935. Although wildfire was considered devastating to most young pine plantations, longleaf pine seedlings and saplings had capability to recover from hot and damaging fires. Evaluations of fire on pine plantations became a common treatment of many research studies.

Fire and longleaf pine management

Fire research began on the experimental forest in the mid-1930s. This work demonstrated that prescribed fire was needed to keep forest rangeland free of woody growth and maintain quality forage for livestock production (Grelen 1976). These fires were also found to benefit longleaf pine regeneration due to the species' tolerance to fire, particularly while in their grass stage period when there is little stem growth. Grass-stage seedlings are susceptible to encroachment by brush and other pine species, smothering by grass and needle litter, and brown-spot needle infection (Wahlenberg 1946). Prescribed burning relieves longleaf seedlings

TOP: *These 10-year-old slash pines were completely defoliated by wildfire. According to Mann and Gunter (1960), heavy mortality will result from this fire.*

BOTTOM: *Dark brown areas extending upward at the base of this tree are dead cambium tissues.*

from these stresses by removing seedling competition and controlling the disease, thereby improving seeding survival (Grelen 1983).

Once longleaf seedlings emerge from the grass stage, they are more susceptible to heat injury. Nevertheless, most longleaf seedlings survive while other woody species are top killed by fire. Based on research on the Palustris Experimental Forest, Grelen (1975) reported that prescribed fire applied biennially in May resulted in larger longleaf pine saplings than such fires in either March or July. He attributed the better growth following May fires to the morphological characteristics of the new shoots.

TOP: Repeated use of fire is needed to control undesirable species and develop a herbaceous understory in longleaf pine forests.

BOTTOM: Fire burned this longleaf pine plantation still in the grass stage. These seedlings will survive the fire and soon initiate height growth.

More recently, Sword Sayer and Haywood (2009) determined that longleaf pine mobilizes starch stored in the roots to support new growth and build foliage. Starch reserves are high in May thereby favoring May as a time to burn with little loss of tree growth. Starch reserves are lower in March and July and relate to poorer response from burning. Intense fires can reduce the growth of longleaf pine saplings and trees although most survive (Haywood 2002).

Predicting mortality of fire-damaged pines
Foresters were uncertain on whether to salvage or replant pines that had much or all their crowns burned during hot fires. Bill Mann of the Southern Station and Erin R. Gunter of the Louisiana Forestry Commission installed studies in the early 1950s to establish guidelines for predicting tree mortality from severe fire damage (Mann and Gunter 1960).

They addressed cambium condition and needle scorch in slash, loblolly, and slash pine stands. Dead cambium was sampled by making small chisel cuts through the bark at four equally spaced locations around the tree. Brown cambium material was determined to be dead. Cambium kill was often in uneven or in fingered streaks.

Needle scorch damage was more closely related to death of trees than was extent of cambium kill. However, mortality was not heavy unless more than 90 percent of the crown was damaged. Trees with less than 50 percent of live crown scorched usually survived even though all four quadrants showed cambium kill at the ground line (Mann and Gunter 1960). They concluded that the proportion of live crown with needle scorch and the extent of cambium kill at the ground line appeared to be better indicators of mortality than height of bark charring, length of live crown with needles consumed, pitch bleeding, or presence of bark beetles.

No longleaf trees were included in this study and young longleaf saplings are known to be more resistant to fire damage than other southern pines. However, knowledge of the resistance of large longleaf trees to fire is not clear. Many organizations now limit the use of prescribed fire due to the damage and mortality that results from hot fires and to the potential negative effect on long-term soil productivity.

Establishment of a fire research work unit
Although research on fire and its effects had been studied by Southern Station scientists for many years, a fire research work unit was established in Pineville when the new facilities were developed in 1964. George R. Fahnestock was named head of the unit—he had been assigned to the Southern Forest Experiment Station since 1957.

George R. Fahnestock led the fire research program in Pineville until fire research was consolidated nationally in 1965.

Fahnestock gained experience in fire behavior during earlier assignments to the Intermountain and Rocky Mountain Forest and Range Experiment Stations. While in the South, he worked primarily with fire issues related to longleaf and loblolly pine.

Shortly after creation of the Fire Research Work Unit, Forest Service Research consolidated its fire research into two major installations: Macon, GA, and Missoula, MT. Fahnestock was reassigned to the Pacific Northwest Forest and Range Experiment Station where he had a long and productive career in fire research.

The formal fire research program in Pineville was closed and needed fire research was carried out by scientists in the Forest and Range Management Research Work Units as part of their ongoing programs.

Incorporating fire into ongoing forest and range research

Although no formal forest fire research program remained, fire effects continued to be integral aspects of forest and range research. The Palustris Experimental Forest was an ideal site for such research because both the Johnson and Longleaf tracts were initially open, cutover land. Use of fire was essential to conduct studies and apply treatments. Much of the enlightenment of fire effects in longleaf forests happened because of the interaction between forest and range research efforts on the forest.

For example, seasonal burning studies installed by range ecologists for evaluating effects of fire on forage development showed that spring burns improved control of undesirable hardwoods and initiation of height growth of longleaf pine. These studies also demonstrated the need for frequent burning to obtain and maintain a desirable longleaf pine ecosystem. Maintaining such joint efforts over time has been productive.

Long-term fire studies

Prescribed burning of southern pine forests helps control hardwoods and increases herbaceous plant production. Effects of a single burn are transitory, so a program of burning is needed to restore longleaf pine

ecosystems and maintain a herbaceous understory. From 1962 through 1998, 20 prescribed burns were applied in a natural stand of longleaf pine to determine the long-term effects of fire regimes on the forest plant community (Haywood and others 2001).

Early in these long-term fire studies, Grelen (1975) reported that biennial burning in May resulted in larger longleaf pine saplings than similar burning in either March or July. The positive aspects of this relationship between May burning and greater longleaf pine development has continued through age 37 years (Haywood and others 2001). The major influence of burning was not, however, on improving long-term pine yield, but on its influence on overall stand structure and species composition.

Another long-term study, evaluating effects of various fire regimes on vegetation in a direct-seeded stand of longleaf pine, was reported after 20 years of treatment (Haywood and Grelen 2000). The 12 prescribed burns conducted during the study increased stocking of longleaf pine over that in the unburned plots. On the burned treatments, longleaf pines were significantly smaller than the unburned trees. Fire effectively kept natural loblolly pine seedlings from reaching sapling size, but loblolly saplings and poles dominated the unburned plots.

The research suggested that land managers face a quandary. To grow longleaf pine and maintain the longleaf ecosystem, rapidly growing and competitive natural loblolly pine must be controlled. Prescribed burning is an effective technique to accomplish this. Frequent and repeated use of fire, however, may deplete nutrients and slow growth of longleaf stands. If land managers want to maintain understory herbaceous and woody vegetation for wildlife habitat and to protect rare or endangered species, reducing the growth to obtain the desired forest cover may be an acceptable outcome (Haywood and Grelen 2000).

Summary of the Research Programs

The scope and nature of research conducted on the Palustris Experimental Forest during the last 75 years is remarkable. The forest was established in 1935 to provide a site for evaluating bareroot nursery practices. Phillip Wakeley's research program moved to the Stuart Nursery in 1934, and nearly 750,000 seedlings were planted in research studies in the next few years. A product of this effort was Wakeley's "Planting the Southern Pines" (1954), which helped guide land managers in regenerating southern pines.

With resumption of research after World War II, artificial regeneration of southern pines continued as a focus of the research program. Using bird and rodent repellents, direct seeding technology was developed to allow rapid reforestation of large areas of open, cutover land. Key to successful reforestation efforts was seed research that provided knowledge to collect, process, treat, and store large quantities of high quality seeds. This technology has been applied not only across the South, but internationally as well.

Efforts to improve bareroot nursery production continued, but successful establishment of longleaf pine remained a significant problem even though physiological studies have clarified the processes. Technology to grow seedlings in small containers was developed and found to greatly improve success of longleaf pine reforestation efforts. Container nursery technology is now used almost exclusively to artificially regenerate longleaf pine.

As old-growth forests were harvested, millions of acres of cutover land became open range for livestock production. As reforestation technology began to be applied, grazing livestock on the land limited success of these efforts. The Longleaf Tract of the Palustris Experimental forest was established in 1950 to provide a resource for conducting range studies that would minimize these conflicting interests. Range research continued for over 40 years and provided guidelines to successfully accommodate use of forest land for livestock production.

As use of forest land for livestock production declined due to economic conditions, range programs transitioned into agroforestry programs that provided

Aerial seeding by plane and helicopter was used to quickly regenerate hundreds of thousands of acres of cutover land.

land managers with scientific information to support multiple uses of forest land, such as pine straw harvesting.

As plantation establishment succeeded, research related to stand management was needed. These studies involved planting spacing; initiation, level, and frequency of thinning; competition control; prescribed burning; and modeling of stand projections. Stand manipulations to optimize growth and yield have been a major effort throughout the existence of the experimental forest and these long-term studies have been measured repeatedly. Hundreds of publications have resulted from these efforts and the results have shaped silvicultural practices applied to southern pine plantations. The databases from these studies have been used to develop models for projecting growth and yield of plantations. Guidelines developed from these studies have been applied across the region.

A key to developing productive plantations was controlling competing scrub hardwood species that grew on much of the cutover land. These species had no economic value and required herbicides to kill them, thus releasing sites for pine growth. Fred Peevy's pioneering research on developing effective chemicals and application techniques was critical in establishing plantations on hundreds of thousands of acres across the South.

Soil-related studies represent long-term research that has regional and national significance. Early in the reforestation era, questions remained related to which species were best suited for planting particular sites. Numerous studies were installed to address this site-species issue, including a wide array of site modification treatments. The largest was Gene Shoulders' "choice of species" study, planted on 113 sites across Louisiana and southern Mississippi. Results of these studies continue to guide planting recommendations across the South.

Another major soil-related study is the long-term soil productivity (LTSP) effort to evaluate the effects of current management practices on growth and productivity of succeeding stand rotations. Initiated on the Experimental Forest, this program has become of national and international significance with study installations across the United States and Canada. Forest industry has installed studies to complement the LTSP effort and develop mitigating measures when operational practices tend to degrade the soil. The goal of this effort is to ensure that forest soil productivity is maintained over time.

Fire-related research continues to be an integral part of programs conducted on the experimental forest. Of particular importance have been studies that document

Tree injectors, developed to insert herbicides into low-quality hardwoods, became a major tool in killing these scrub trees.

the long-term effects of prescribed fire on restoration and management of longleaf pine ecosystems. These results have become incorporated into longleaf pine management systems that have been adopted across the South.

Numerous research studies and programs have been installed on the experimental forest with the goal of improving plantation establishment success and on increasing stand growth and yield. These have taken many forms from site preparation, prescribed fire, fertilization, stand manipulation, and competition control to tree improvement, genetics, insect studies, and disease control. For decades, these research efforts have succeeded in providing management tools to establish stands and to maintain and enhance southern forest productivity.

Conclusions

For 75 years, the Palustris Experimental Forest has been used as a site for studies in forest management, range research, and intensive silviculture research. The scope of the research has been extraordinary, and its focus on interacting resource values was in place long before there were emphases to do so. Studies on the Palustris Experimental Forest have provided a vital link to multiple-use management of natural resources across the South, providing much of the ecological basis for managing Federal, State, and private lands.

Nearly 2,000 publications of research associated with the Palustris Experimental Forest document the extent to which this research provides the basis for establishment and management of pine plantations across the South and around the world where southern pines have been introduced. One reason for the scope and productivity of the research programs was co-location and collaboration, not only among scientists of numerous disciplines but also among specialists from the forest industry, universities, State and private forests, and the National Forest System.

In a broader perspective, these research programs have had an enormous effect on the economy of the South. Seventy-five years ago, forestry in the South was in its infancy, with much of the South's forests in a decimated condition and with little information available on how to restore this cutover land to a productive state. Carter and Foster (2006) document that in 1950, pine plantations accounted for less than 1 percent of the area of southern forests, but by 1999, plantations covered 30 million acres or 15 percent of the South's timberland and nearly 50 percent of all pine forests. Much of the research that provided the technology for reforestation and stand productivity was developed from programs conducted on the Palustris Experimental Forest. Related technologies from a number of disciplines have supplemented this effort and provided compatible ecological and environmental management systems. Application of this research led the effort to make the South's forests the most productive in the world and the practice of forestry now drives the economy of most Southern States.

Technology to restore cutover land into productive forests has resulted from the research programs that have been conducted on the Palustris Experimental Forest.

Literature Cited

Baldwin, V.C., Jr. 1987. Green and dry-weight equations for aboveground components of planted loblolly pine trees in the West Gulf Region. Southern Journal of Applied Forestry. 11: 212-218.

Baldwin, V.C., Jr.; Burkhart, H.E.; Dougherty, P.M.; Teskey, R.O. 1993. Using a growth and yield model (PTAEDA2) as a driver for a biological process model (MAESTRO). Res. Pap. SO-276. New Orleans: U.S. Department of Agriculture Forest Service, Southern Forest Experiment Station. 9 p.

Baldwin, V.C., Jr.; Burkhart, H.E.; Westfall, J.A.; Peterson, K.D. 2001. Linking growth and yield and process models to estimate impact of environmental changes on growth of loblolly pine. Forest Science. 47: 77-82.

Baldwin, V.C., Jr.; Cao, Q.V. 1999. Modeling forest timber productivity in the south: Where are we today? In: Haywood, J.D., ed. Proceedings of the 10th biennial southern silvicultural research conference. Gen. Tech. Rep. SRS-30. Asheville, NC: U.S. Department of Agriculture Forest Service, Southern Research Station: 487-496.

Baldwin, V.C., Jr.; Dougherty, P.M.; Burkhart, H.E. 1998. A linked model for stimulating stand development and growth processes of loblolly pine. In: Mickler, R.A.; Fox, S. The productivity and sustainability of southern forest ecosystems in a changing environment. New York: Springer-Verlag: 305-325.

Baldwin, V.C., Jr.; Feduccia, D.P. 1987. Loblolly pine growth and yield prediction of managed West Gulf plantations. Res. Pap. SO-236. New Orleans: U.S. Department of Agriculture Forest Service, Southern Forest Experiment Station. 27 p.

Baldwin, V.C., Jr.; Feduccia, D.P. 1991. Compatible tree-volume and upper-stem diameter equations for plantation loblolly pine in the West Gulf Region. Southern Journal of Applied Forestry. 16: 92-97.

Baldwin, V.C., Jr.; Feduccia, D.P.; Haywood, J.D. 1989. Postthinning growth and yield of row-thinned and selectively thinned loblolly and slash pine plantations. Canadian Journal of Forest Research. 19: 247-256.

Baldwin, V.C., Jr.; Leduc, D.J.; Ferguson, R.B. [and others]. 1998. The not-so-sudden results of the sudden saw log study—growth and yield through age 45. In: Waldrop, T.A., ed. Proceedings of the 9th biennial southern silvicultural research conference. Gen. Tech. Rep. SRS-20. Asheville, NC: U.S. Department of Agriculture Forest Service, Southern Research Station: 574-578.

Baldwin, V.C., Jr.; Peterson, K.D.; Clark, A., III. [and others]. 2000. The effects of thinning on stand and tree characteristics of 38-year-old loblolly pine. Forest Ecology and Management. 137: 91-102.

Baldwin, V.C., Jr.; Polmer, B.H. 1981. Taper functions for unthinned longleaf pine plantations on cutover sites. In: Barnett, J.P., ed. Proceedings of the 1st biennial southern silvicultural research conference. Gen. Tech. Rep. SO-34. New Orleans: U.S. Department of Agriculture Forest Service, Southern Forest Experiment Station: 156-163.

Barnett, J.P.. 1969. Long-term storage of longleaf pine seeds. Tree Planters' Notes. 20(2): 22-25.

Barnett, J.P. 1970. Storage of sand pine seeds. Tree Planters' Notes. 21(4): 11-12.

Barnett, J.P. 1971. Aerated water soaks stimulate germination of southern pine seeds. Res. Pap. S0-67. New Orleans: U.S. Department of Agriculture Forest Service, Southern Forest Experiment Station. 9 p.

Barnett, J.P. 1972. Seedcoat influences dormancy of loblolly pine seeds. Canadian Journal of Forest Research. 2: 7-10.

Barnett, J.P. 1976a. Cone and seed maturation of southern pine. Res. Pap. SO-122. New Orleans: U.S. Department of Agriculture Forest Service, Southern Forest Experiment Station. 11 p.

Barnett, J.P. 1976b. Delayed germination of southern pine seeds related to seed coat constraint. Canadian Journal of Forest Research. 6: 504-510.

Barnett, J.P.. 1976c. Sterilizing southern pine seeds with hydrogen peroxide. Tree Planters' Notes. 27(3): 17-19, 24.

Barnett, J.P. 1980. Density and age affect performance of containerized loblolly pine seedlings. Res. Note SO-256. New Orleans: U.S. Department of Agriculture Forest Service, Southern Forest Experiment Station. 5 p.

Barnett, J.P. 1983. Relating field performance of containerized longleaf and shortleaf pine seedlings to mycorrhizal inoculation and initial size. In: Proceedings, 7th North American Forest Biology Workshop. Lexington, KY: University of Kentucky: 358-367.

Barnett, J.P. 1984. Relating seedling physiology to survival and growth in container grown southern pines. In: M.L. Duryea; Brown, G N., eds. Seedling Physiology and Reforestation Success. Dordrecht, Netherlands: Martinus Nijhoff/Dr. W. Junk Publishers: 157-176

Barnett, J.P. 1988. Eastern white pine cone and seed maturity in the Southern Appalachians. Northern Journal of Applied Forestry. 5: 172-176.

Barnett, J.P. 1991. Seedbed densities and sowing and lifting dates affect nursery development and field survival of longleaf pine seedlings. Tree Planters' Notes. 42(3): 28- 29.

Barnett, J.P. 1993. Presowing treatments affect shortleaf pine seed germination and seedling development. Tree Planters' Notes. 44(2): 58-62.

Barnett, J.P.; Bergman, P.W.; Ferguson, W.L. [and others]. 1980. The biologic and economic assessment of endrin. Cooperative Impact Assessment Report. Tech. Bulletin 1623. Washington: U.S. Department of Agriculture. 47 p.

Barnett, J.P.; Brissette, J.C. 1986. Producing southern pine seedlings in containers. Gen. Tech. Rep. SO-59. New Orleans: U.S. Department of Agriculture Forest Service, Southern Forest Experiment Station. 71 p.

Barnett, J.P.; Brissette, J.C. 2004. Stock type affects performance of shortleaf pine planted in the Ouachita Mountains through 10 years. In: Connor, K., ed. Proceedings of the 12th biennial southern silvicultural research conference. Gen. Tech. Rep. SRS-71. Asheville, NC: U.S. Department of Agriculture Forest Service, Southern Research Station: 420-422.

Barnett, J.P.; Brissette, J.C. 2007. Regenerating shortleaf pine: results of a 5-year cooperative research initiative. In: Kabrick, J.M.; Dey, D.C.; Gwaze, E., eds. Shortleaf pine restoration and ecology in the Ozarks: Proceedings of a symposium. Gen. Tech. Rep. NRS-P-15. Newtown Square, PA: U.S. Department of Agriculture Forest Service, Northern Research Station: 105-111.

Barnett, J.P.; Brissette, J.C.; Kais, A.G. [and others]. 1988. Improving field performance of southern pine seedlings by treating with fungicides before storage. Southern Journal of Applied Forestry. 12: 281-285.

Barnett, J.P.; Dumroese, R.K.; Moorhead, D.J. 2002a. Proceedings of workshops on growing longleaf pine in containers—1999 and 2001. Gen. Tech. Rep. SRS-56. Asheville, NC: U.S. Department of Agriculture Forest Service, Southern Research Station. 63 p.

Barnett, J.P.; Hainds, M.J.; Hernandez, G.A. 2002b. Interim guidelines for growing longleaf pine seedlings in containers. [Brochure]. Gen. Tech. Rep. SRS-60. Asheville, NC: U.S. Department of Agriculture Forest Service, Southern Research Station.

Barnett, J.P.; Kais, A.G. 1987. Longleaf pine storability and resistance to brown-spot disease improved by adding benomyl to the packing medium. In: Phillips, D.R., comp. Proceedings of the 4th biennial southern silvicultural research conference. Gen. Tech. Rep. SE-42. Asheville, NC: U.S. Department of Agriculture Forest Service, Southeastern Forest Experiment Station: 222-224.

Barnett, J.P.; Krugman, S.L. 1989. Electromagnetic treatment of loblolly pine seeds. Res. Note SO-356. New Orleans: U.S. Department of Agriculture Forest Service, Southern Forest Experiment Station. 7 p.

Barnett, J.P.; McGilvray, J.M. 1981. Container planting systems for the South. Res. Pap. SO-167. New Orleans: U.S. Department of Agriculture Forest Service, Southern Forest Experiment Station. 18 p.

Barnett, J.P.; McGilvray, J.M. 1993. Performance of container and bareroot loblolly pine seedlings on bottomlands in South Carolina. Southern Journal of Applied Forestry. 17: 80-83.

Barnett, J.P.; McGilvray, J.M. 1997. Practical guidelines for producing longleaf pine seedlings in containers. Gen. Tech. Rep. SRS-14. Asheville, NC: U.S. Department of Agriculture Forest Service, Southern Research Station. 28 p.

Barnett, J.P.; McGilvray, J.M. 2002a. Guidelines for producing quality longleaf pine seeds. Gen. Tech. Rep. SRS-52. Asheville, NC: U.S. Department of Agriculture, Forest Service, Southern Research Station. 21 p.

Barnett, J.P.; McGilvray, J.M. 2002b. Improving longleaf pine seedling production by controlling seed and seedling pathogens. In: Outcalt, K.W., ed. Proceedings of the 11th biennial southern silvicultural research conference. Gen. Tech. Rep. SRS-48. Asheville, NC: U.S. Department of Agriculture Forest Service, Southern Research Station: 45-46.

Barnett, J.P.; McLemore, B.F. 1970. Storing southern pine seeds. Journal of Forestry. 68: 24-27.

Barnett, J.P.; McLemore, B.F. 1984. Germination speed as a predictor of seedling performance. Southern Journal of Applied Forestry. 8: 157-162.

Barnett, J.; Pickens, B.; Karrfalt, R. 1999. Longleaf pine seed presowing treatments: effects on germination and nursery establishment. In: Landis, T.D; Barnett, J.P., tech. coords. National Proceedings: Forest and Conservation Nursery Association—1998. Gen. Tech Rep. SRS-25. Asheville, NC: U.S. Department of Agriculture Forest Service, Southern Research Station: 43-46.

Barnett, J.P.; Vozzo, J.A. 1985. Viability and vigor of slash and shortleaf pine seeds after 50 years of storage. Forest Science. 31: 316-320.

Boyer, W.D. 1987. Volume growth loss: A hidden cost of periodic prescribed burning in longleaf pine? Southern Journal of Applied Forestry. 11: 154-157.

Brady, H.A. 1975. Aspects of dicamba behavior in woody plants. Southern Weed Science Society. 28: 236-243.

Brady, H.A.; Hall, O. 1976. Relation of sugar changes and herbicides susceptibility in woody plants. Southern Weed Science Society. 29: 276-283.

Brissette, J.C.; Barnett, J.P. 1989. Depth of planting and J-rooting affect loblolly pine seedlings under stress. In: Miller, J.H., ed. Proceedings 5th biennial southern silvicultural research conference. Gen. Tech. Rep. SO-74. New Orleans: U.S. Department of Agriculture Forest Service, Southern Forest Experiment Station: 169-175.

Brissette, J.C.; Barnett, J.P. 1992. Proceedings of the shortleaf pine regeneration workshop. Gen. Tech. Rep. SO-90. New Orleans: U.S. Department of Agriculture Forest Service, Southern Forest Experiment Station. 236 p.

Brissette, J.C.; Barnett, J.P. 1993. Lifting date and storage duration affect root growth potential and field survival of shortleaf pine seedlings from three geographic sources and two nurseries. In: Brissette, J.C., ed. Proceedings of the 7th biennial southern silvicultural research conference. Gen. Tech. Rep. SO-93. New Orleans: U.S. Department of Agriculture, Forest Service, Southern Forest Experiment Station: 263-268.

Brissette, J.C.: Barnett, J.P.; Flagler, R.B. 1994. Root zone environment affects new root growth of shortleaf pine seedlings from East Texas. In: Forest biodiversity in a changing environment. North American forest biology workshop. Baton Rouge, LA: Louisiana State University, Agricultural Center: 31.

Brissette, J.C.; Barnett, J.P.; Gramling, C.L. 1988. Root growth potential of southern pine seedlings grown at the W.W. Ashe nursery. In: Proceedings, Southern Forest Nursery Association Meeting. Columbia, SC: Southern Forest Nursery Association: 173-183.

Brissette, J.C.; Barnett, J.P.; Jones, J.P. 1996. Fungicides improve field performance of stored loblolly and longleaf pine seedlings. Southern Journal of Applied Forestry. 20: 5-9.

Brissette, J.C.; Barnett, J.P.; Landis, T.D. 1991. Container seedlings. Chapter 7 in Duryea, M.L ; Dougherty, P.M., eds. Forest regeneration manual. Dordrecht, The Netherlands: Kluwer Academic Publishers: 117-141.

Brissette, J.C.; Carlson, W.C. 1987. Effects of nursery bed density and fertilization on the morphology, nutrient status, and root growth potential of shortleaf pine seedlings. In: Phillips, D.R., comp. Proceedings 4th biennial southern silvicultural research conference. Gen. Tech. Rep. SE-42. Asheville, NC: U.S. Department of Agriculture Forest Service, Southeastern Forest Research Station: 198-205.

Brissette, J.C.; Chambers, J.L. 1992. Leaf water status and root system water flux of shortleaf pine (Pinus echinata Mill.) seedlings in relation to new root growth after transplanting. Tree Physiology. 11: 289-303.

Burton, J.D. 1982. Sawtimber by prescription—the sudden sawlog story through age 33. Res. Pap. SO-179. New Orleans: U.S. Department of Agriculture Forest Service, Southern Forest Experiment Station. 9 p.

Burton, J.D.; Shoulders, E. 1974. Fast-grown, dense loblolly pine sawlogs. Journal of Forestry. 72(10): 637-641.

Burton, J.D.; Shoulders, E ; Snow, G.A. 1985. Incidence and impact of fusiform rust vary with silviculture in slash pine plantations. Forest Science. 31: 671-680.

Burton, J.D.; Snow, G.A. 1983. Triadimefon controls fusiform rust in young pine outplantings. Plant Disease. 67: 853-854.

Busby, R.L ; Ward, K B.; Baldwin, V.C., Jr. 1990. COMPUTE_ MERCHLOB: a growth and yield prediction system with a merchandizing optimizer for planted loblolly pine in the West Gulf Region. Res. Note SO-255. New Orleans: U.S. Department of Agriculture, Forest Service, Southern Forest Experiment Station. 22 p.

Byrd, N.A.; Lewis, C.E.; Pearson, H.A. 1984. Management of southern pine forests for cattle production. Gen. Rep. R8-GR-4. Atlanta: U.S. Department of Agriculture, Southern Region. 22 p.

Campbell, T.E. 1976. The Nation's oldest industrial direct seeding. Forests & People. 26(3): 22-24.

Cao, Q.V.; Baldwin, V.C., Jr. 1999. A new algorithm for stand projection models. Forest Science. 45: 406-511.

Cao, Q.V.; Dean, T.J.; Baldwin, V.C., Jr. 1999. Modeling the size-density relationship in direct-seeded slash pine stands. Forest Science. 46: 317-321.

Carter, M.C.; Foster, C.D. 2006. Milestones and millstones: A retrospective on 50 years of research to improve productivity in loblolly pine plantations. Forest Ecology and Management. 227: 137-144.

Cassady, J.T.; Hopkins, W.; Whitaker, L.B. 1955. Cattle grazing damage to pine seedlings. Occasional Paper 141. New Orleans: U.S. Department of Agriculture Forest Service, Southern Forest Experiment Station. 14 p.

Cassady, J.T.; Mann, W.F., Jr. 1954. The Alexandria Research Center. Misc. Pub. New Orleans: U.S. Department of Agriculture Forest Service, Southern Forest Experiment Station. 26 p.

Cassady, J.T.; Shepherd, W.O. 1949. Grazing on forested lands. In: 1948 Yearbook of Agriculture. Washington: U.S. Government Printing Office: 468-472.

Chambers, J.L.; Clifton, R.G.P.; Barnett, J.P. 1988. Sand culture and raised beds for inducement of water stress in seedling physiology studies. In: Worrall, J ; Loo-Dinkins, J.; D. Lester, T., eds. Proceedings, 10th North American Forest Biology Workshop. Vancouver, BC: British Columbia Forest Service: 164-168.

Czabator, F.J.; Enghardt, H. 1959. Nursery-infected seedlings develop rust cankers after outplanting. Tree Planter's Notes. Washington: U.S. Department of Agriculture Forest Service 37: 23-25.

Dean, T.J.; Baldwin, V.C., Jr. 1993. Using a density-management diagram to develop thinning schedules for loblolly pine plantations. Res. Pap. SO-275. New Orleans: U.S. Department of Agriculture Forest Service, Southern Forest Experiment Station. 7 p.

Dell, T.R.; Feduccia, D.P.; Campbell, T.E. [and others]. 1979. Yields of unthinned slash pine plantation on cutover sites in the West Gulf Region. Res. Pap. SO-147. New Orleans: U.S. Department of Agriculture Forest Service, Southern Forest Experiment Station. 84 p.

Dell, T.; Koretz, J.; Shoulders, E. 1989. Progress on shortleaf plantation, data pool and growth predictions. In: Miller, J.H., ed. Proceeding of the 5th biennial southern silvicultural conference. Gen. Tech. Rep. SO-74. New Orleans: U.S. Department of Agriculture Forest Service, Southern Forest Experiment Station: 441-445.

Derr, H.J. 1964. New repellent formulation for direct seeding. Journal of Forestry. 62: 265.

Derr, H.J. 1966. Longleaf x slash hybrids at age 7: Survival, growth, and disease susceptibility. Journal of Forestry. 64: 236-239.

Derr, H.J.; Mann, W.F., Jr. 1953. Cost of pruning longleaf pine. Journal of Forestry. 51(8): 579.

Derr, H.J.; Mann, W.F., Jr. 1971. Direct-seeding pines in the South. Agric. Handb. 391. Washington: U.S. Department of Agriculture, Forest Service. 67 p.

Derr, H.J.; Mann, W.F., Jr. 1977. Bedding poorly drained sites for planting loblolly and slash pines. Res. Pap. SO-134. New Orleans: U.S. Department of Agriculture Southern Forest Experiment Station. 4 p.

Derr, H.J.; Melder T.W. 1970. Brown-spot resistance in longleaf pine. Forest Science. 16: 204-209.

Dumroese, R.K.; Barnett, J.P.; Jackson, D.P.; Hainds, M. 2009. 2008 interim guidelines for growing longleaf pine seedlings in container nurseries. In: Dumroese, R.K.; Riley, L E., tech. coord. National proceedings: forest and conservation nursery associations—2008. Proceedings RMRS-P-58. Fort Collins, CO: U.S. Department of Agriculture Forest Service, Rocky Mountain Research Station: 101-107.

Dumroese, R.K; Landis, T.D.; Barnett, J.P.; Burch, F. 2005. Forest Service nurseries: 100 years of ecosystem restoration. Journal of Forestry. 103(5): 241-247.

Dumroese, R.K.; Landis, T.D.; Luna, T.; Hernandez, G. 2008. Simple methods for raising tree and shrub seedlings in Afghanistan. Washington: U.S. Agency for International Development and U.S. Department of Agriculture, Foreign Agriculture Service, Office of Capacity Building and Development. 63 p.

Dumroese, R.K.; Luna, T.; Landis, T. 2009. Nursery manual for native plants: A guide for tribal nurseries—Volume 1: Nursery management. Agric. Handb. 730. Washington: U.S. Department of Agriculture Forest Service. 302 p.

Duvall, V.L.; Linnartz, N.E. 1967. Influences of grazing and fire on vegetation and soil of longleaf pine-bluestem range. Journal of Range Management. 20(4): 241-247.

Duvall, V.L.; Whitaker, L.B. 1964. Rotation burning: A forage management system for longleaf pine-bluestem ranges. Journal of Range Management. 17(6): 322-326.

Echols, H.W. 1965. Town ants controlled with Mirex baits. Res. Note SO-18. New Orleans: U.S. Department of Agriculture Forest Service, Southern Forest Experiment Station. 2 p.

Echols, H.W. 1966. Texas leaf-cutting ants controlled with pelleted Mirex bait. Journal of Economic Entomology. 19: 628-631.

Enghardt, H.G.; Smith, L.F.; Wells, O.O. 1969. Pruning to reduce fusiform-rust damage not justified on young slash pines. Res. Note SO-87. New Orleans: U.S. Department of Agriculture Forest Service, Southern Forest Experiment Station. 3 p.

Feduccia, D.P. 1983. Thinning pine plantations. Forest Farmer. XLII(10): 10-11.

Feduccia, D.P.; Dell, T.R.; Mann, W.F., Jr. [and others]. 1979. Yields of unthinned loblolly pine plantations on cutover sites in the West Gulf Region. Res. Pap. SO-148. New Orleans: U.S. Department of Agriculture Forest Service, Southern Forest Experiment Station. 88 p.

Feduccia, D.; Mosier, J. 1977. The Woodworth spacing and thinning study: An obituary. Forests & People. 27(1): 18-21.

Ferguson, R.B.; Baldwin, V.C., Jr. 1987. Comprehensive outlook for managed pines using simulated treatment experiments-planted loblolly pine (COMPUTE_P-LOB): A user's guide. Res. Pap. SO-241. New Orleans: U.S. Department of Agriculture Forest Service, Southern Forest Experiment Station. 64 p.

Ferguson, R.B.; Baldwin, V.C., Jr. 1995. Spacing effects on unthinned slash pine in the West Gulf. In: Edwards, M.B., comp. Proceedings of the 8th biennial southern silvicultural research conference. Gen. Tech. Rep. SRS-1. Asheville, NC: U.S. Department of Agriculture Forest Service, Southern Research Station: 473-478.

Fleming, R.L.; Powers, R.F.; Foster, N.W. [and others]. 2006. Effects of organic removal, soil compaction, and vegetation control on 5-year seedling performance: A regional comparison of long-term soil productivity sites. Canadian Journal of Forest Research. 36: 529-550.

Fox, T.R ; Jokela, E.J.; Allen, H.L. 2007. The development of pine plantation silviculture in the Southern United States. Journal of Forestry. 105: 337-347.

Grelen, H.E. 1975. Vegetative response to twelve years of seasonal burning on a Louisiana longleaf pine site. Res. Note SO-192. New Orleans: U.S. Department of Agriculture Forest Service, Southern Forest Experiment Station. 4 p.

Grelen, H.E. 1976. Responses of herbage, pines, and hardwoods to early and delayed burning in a young pine slash pine plantation. Journal of Range Management. 29(4): 301-303.

Grelen, H.E. 1978. Forest grazing in the South. Journal of Range Management. 31(4): 244-250

Grelen, H.E. 1983. May burning favors survival and early height growth of longleaf pine seedlings. Southern Journal of Applied Forestry. 7: 16-19.

Grelen, H.E ; Duvall, V.L. 1966. Common plants of longleaf pine-bluestem range. Res. Pap. SO-23. New Orleans: U.S. Department of Agriculture Forest Service, Southern Forest Experiment Station. 100 p.

Grelen, H.E.; Epps, E.A., Jr. 1967. Season of burning affects herbage quality and yield on pine-bluestem range. Journal of Range Management. 20(1): 31-33.

Grelen, H.E.; Pearson, H.A. 1977. Liquid supplements for cattle on southern forest range. Journal of Range Management. 30: 94-96.

Grelen, H.E.; Pearson, H.A.; Thill, R.E. 1985. Establishment and growth of slash pine on grazed cutover range in central Louisiana. Southern Journal of Applied Forestry. 9(4): 232-236.

Guldin, R.W.; Barnett, J.P. 1982. Proceedings of the southern containerized forest tree seedling conference. Gen. Tech. Rep. SO-37. New Orleans: U.S. Department of Agriculture Forest Service, Southern Forest Experiment Station. 156 p.

Hall, O. 1973. Limitations of surfactant and pH effects on herbicide behavior in woody plants. Weed Science. 21(3): 221-223.

Hallgren, S.W.; Tauer, C.G. 1989. Root growth potential, first-year survival, and growth of shortleaf pine seedlings show efforts of lift date, storage, and family. Southern Journal of Applied Forestry. 13: 163-169.

Haywood, J.D. 1981. Discontinuous mounding as a site treatment on a flatwoods site. In: Barnett, J.P, ed. Proceedings of the 1st biennial southern silvicultural research conference. Gen. Tech. Rep. SO-34. New Orleans: U.S. Department of Agriculture Forest Service, Southern Forest Experiment Station: 50-53.

Haywood, J.D. 1983. Response of planted pines to site preparation on a Beauregard-Caddo soil. In: Jones, E.P., Jr., ed. Proceedings 2nd biennial southern silviculture conference. Gen. Tech. Rep. SE-24. Asheville, NC: U.S. Department of Agriculture Forest Service, Southeastern Forest Experiment Station: 14-17.

Haywood, J.D. 1993. Stripping of soil-applied hexazinone, picloram, and tibuthiuron for loblolly pine site preparation. Res. Note SO-372. New Orleans: U.S. Department of Agriculture Forest Service, Southern Forest Experiment Station. 6 p.

Haywood, J.D. 1994. Seasonal and cumulative loblolly pine development under two stand density and fertility levels through four growing seasons. Res. Pap. SO-283. New Orleans: U.S. Department of Agriculture Forest Service, Southern Forest Experiment Station. 5 p.

Haywood, J.D. 1995. Controlling herbaceous competition in pasture planted with loblolly pine seedlings. Res. Note SO-381. New Orleans: U.S. Department of Agriculture Forest Service, Southern Forest Experiment Station. 8 p.

Haywood, J.D. 2000. Mulch and hexazinone herbicide shorten the time longleaf pine seedlings are in the grass stage and increase height growth. New Forests. 19: 279-290.

Haywood, J.D. 2002. Delayed prescribed burning in a seedling and sapling longleaf pine plantation in Louisiana. In: Outcalt, K.W., ed. Proceedings of the 11th biennial silvicultural research conference. Gen. Tech. Rep. SRS-48. Asheville, NC: U.S. Department of Agriculture, Forest Service, Southern Research Station: 103-108.

Haywood, J.D. 2005. Effects of herbaceous and woody plant control on Pinus palustris growth and foliar nutrients through six growing seasons. Forest Ecology and Management. 214: 384-397.

Haywood, J.D. 2007. Influence of herbicides and felling, fertilization, and prescribed fire on longleaf pine establishment and growth through six growing seasons. New Forests. 33: 257-279.

Haywood, J.D. 2009. Eight years of seasonal burning and herbicidal brush control influence sapling longleaf pine growth, understory vegetation, and the outcome of an ensuing wildfire. Forest Ecology and Management. 258: 296-305.

Haywood, J.D.; Elliott-Smith, M.; Knight, R. [and others]. 1996. Harvesting longleaf pine straw on the Kisatchie National Forest. In: Kush, J.S., comp. Longleaf pine: a regional perspective of challenges and opportunities. Proceeding 1st Longleaf Alliance Conference. Mobile, AL: University of Alabama, The Longleaf Alliance: 90-92.

Haywood, J.D.; Goelz, J.C.; Sword Sayer, M.A.; Tiarks, A.E. 2003. Influence of fertilization, weed control, and pine litter on loblolly pine growth and productivity and understory plant development through 12 growing seasons. Canadian Journal of Forest Research. 33: 1974-1982.

Haywood, J.D.; Grelen, H.E. 2000. Twenty years of prescribed burning influence the development of direct-seeded longleaf pine on a wet pine site in Louisiana. Southern Journal of Applied Forestry. 24(2): 86-92.

Haywood, J.D.; Harris, F.L.; Grelen, H.E; Pearson, H.A. 2001. Vegetative response to 37 years of seasonal burning on a Louisiana longleaf pine site. Southern Journal of Applied Forestry. 25: 122-130.

Haywood, J.D.; Knight, R.A.; Tiarks, A.E.; Pearson, H.A. 1995. Effects of pine straw harvesting on longleaf pine productivity, nutrition, and forest soil properties. In: Ehrenreich, J.H.; Ehrenreich, D.L.; Lee, H.W., eds. Growing a sustainable future. Proceedings of the fourth North American agroforestry conference; Boise, ID. Moscow, ID: University of Idaho: 51-53.

Haywood, J.D.; Melder, T.W. 1991. Effectiveness of glyphosate mixed with soil-active herbicides. Res. Note SO-365. New Orleans: U.S. Department of Agriculture, Forest Service, Southern Research Station. 5 p.

Haywood, J.D.; Sword, M.A.; Harris, F.L. 2004. Fire monitoring: effects of scorch in Louisiana's pine forests. In: Connor, K F., ed. Proceedings of the 12th biennial silvicultural research conference. Gen. Tech. Rep. SRS-71. Asheville, NC: U.S. Department of Agriculture, Forest Service, Southern Research Station: 65-67.

Haywood, J.D.; Tiarks, A.E. 1990. Eleventh-year results of fertilization, herbaceous, and woody plant control in a loblolly pine plantation. Southern Journal of Applied Forestry. 14: 173-177.

Haywood, J.D.; Tiarks, A.E. 1995. Growth reductions in short-rotation loblolly and slash pines in central Louisiana—10th year results. In: Edwards, M.B., comp. Proceedings of the 8th biennial silvicultural research conference. Gen. Tech. Report SRS-1. Asheville, NC: U.S. Department of Agriculture, Forest Service, Southern Research Station: 268-274.

Haywood, J.D.; Tiarks, A.E.; Snow, G.A. 1994. Combinations of fungicide and cultural practices influence the incidence and impact of fusiform rust in slash pine plantations. Southern Journal of Applied Forestry. 18: 53-59.

Hopkins, W.S. 1948. Hogs or logs! Naval Stores Review. 57(3): 12-13.

Johnston, H.R. 1944. Control of the Texas leaf-cutting ant with methyl bromide. Journal of Forestry. 42: 130-132.

Jokela, E.J.; Martin, T.A.; Vogel, J.G. 2010. Twenty-five years of intensive forest management with southern pines: Important lessons learned. Journal of Forestry. 108(7): 338-347.

Jones, J.P.; Barnett, J.P.; McGilvray, J. 1999. Root rot of container grown longleaf pine seedlings caused by Fusarium circinatum. [Abstract]. Louisiana Plant Protection Association Proceedings. Baton Rouge, LA: Louisiana State University, AgCenter Research and Development: 4.

Jones, J.P.; Pantone, D.J.; Barnett, J.P.; Brissette, J.C. 1992. The relationship between fungal population development and root damage of cold-stored longleaf pine seedlings. Louisiana State University Agricultural Center Bulletin No. 832. Baton Rouge, LA: Louisiana Agricultural Experiment Station. 23 p.

Jones, J.P.; Sun, X.; Barnett, J.P. 1997. Biological control of Pythiaceous fungi causing death to longleaf pine seedlings in cold storage. In: Proceedings, 1997 Annual International Research Conference on Methyl Bromide Alternatives and Emissions Reductions. Washington, DC: Office of Methyl Bromide Alternatives Outreach: 26-1–26-4.

Jones, J.P.; Sun, X.; Eckhardt, L. [and others]. 2002. Longleaf seedling production: Some problems and their solutions. Louisiana Agriculture. 45(3): 4-6.

Kais, A.G. 1989. Brown spot needle blight. In: Cordell, C.E.; Anderson, R.L.; Hoffard, W.H ; [and others], tech. coords. Forest nursery pests. Agric. Handb. 680. Washington: U.S. Department of Agriculture Forest Service: 26-28.

Kuehler, E.A.; Sword Sayer, M.A.; Andries, C.D. 2006. How does fire affect longleaf pine root carbohydrates, foliar nutrients, and sapling growth? In: Connor, K F., ed. Proceedings of the 13th biennial southern silvicultural research conference. Gen. Tech. Rep. SRS-92. Asheville, NC: U.S. Department of Agriculture Forest Service, Southern Research Station: 98-101.

Kuehler, E.A.; Sword-Sayer, M.A.; Haywood, J.D.; Andries, C.D. 2004. Long-term effects of season of prescribed burn on the fine-root growth, root carbohydrates, and foliar dynamics of mature longleaf pine. In: Connor, K.F., ed. Proceedings of the 12th biennial southern silvicultural research conference. Gen. Tech. Rep. SRS-71. Asheville, NC: U.S. Department of Agriculture Forest Service, Southern Research Station: 68-70.

Landis, T.D.; Dreesen, D.R.; Pinto, J.R.; Dumroese, R.K. 2005. Propagating native plants for the Hopi Nation. Combined Proceedings International Plant Propagators' Society. 55: 520-623.

Landis, T.D.; Dumroese, R.K.; Haase, D.L. 2009. The container tree nursery manual: Volume 7, Seedling processing, storage, and outplanting. Agric. Handb. 674. Washington: U.S. Department of Agriculture Forest Service. 199 p.

Leduc, D.J. 2006. PINVOL: A user's guide to a volume calculator for southern pines. Gen. Tech. Rep. SRS-95. Asheville, NC: U.S. Department of Agriculture Forest Service, Southern Research Station. 12 p.

Leduc, D.J.; Goelz, J. 2009. A height-diameter curve for longleaf pine plantations in the Gulf Coastal Plain. Southern Journal of Applied Forestry. 33: 164-170.

Leduc, D.J.; Zeide, B. 1986. The effect of thinning and pruning on the growth of planted loblolly pine stands. In: Phillips, D.R., ed. Proceedings of the 4th biennial southern silvicultural research conference. Gen. Tech. Rep. SE-42. Asheville, NC: U.S. Department of Agriculture, Forest Service, Southeastern Forest Experiment Station: 473-482.

Linnartz, N.D.; Hse, C.Y.; Duvall, V.L. 1966. Grazing impairs physical properties of a forest soil in central Louisiana. Journal of Forestry. 64: 239-243.

Lohrey, R.E. 1972. Precommerical thinning of direct-seeded loblolly pine. Res. Note SO-139. New Orleans: U.S. Department of Agriculture Forest Service, Southern Forest Experiment Station. 4 p.

Lohrey, R.E. 1973. Precommerical thinning increases diameter and height growth of slash pine. Res. Note SO-152. New Orleans: U.S. Department of Agriculture Forest Service, Southern Forest Experiment Station. 4 p.

Lohrey, R.E. 1974. Site preparation improves survival and growth of direct-seeded pines. Res. Note SO-185. New Orleans: U.S. Department of Agriculture Southern Forest Experiment Station. 4 p.

Lohrey, R.E. 1977. Growth responses of loblolly pine to commercial thinning. Southern Journal of Applied Forestry. 1: 19-22.

Lohrey, R.E. 1983. Stem volume prediction and crown characteristics of thinned longleaf pine plantations. In: Jones, E.P., Jr., ed. Proceedings of the 2nd biennial silvicultural research conference. Gen. Tech. Rep. SE-24. Asheville, NC: U.S. Department of Agriculture Forest Service, Southeastern Forest Experiment Station: 338-343.

Lohrey, R.E. 1985. Stem volume, volume ratio, and taper equations for slash pine in the West Gulf Region. In: Shoulders, E., ed. Proceedings of the 3rd biennial silvicultural research conference. Gen. Tech. Rep. SO-54. New Orleans: U.S. Department of Agriculture Forest Service, Southern Forest Experiment Station: 451-459.

Lohrey, R.E. 1987. Site index curves for direct-seeded slash pines in Louisiana. Southern Journal of Applied Forestry. 11: 15-17.

Luna, T.; Landis, T.D.; Pinto, J. 2003. Intertribal nursery council tribal needs assessment. Asheville, NC: U.S. Department of Agriculture Forest Service, Southern Research Station. 85 p.

Lundgren, G.K.; Conner, J.R.; Pearson, H.A. 1983. An economic analysis of forest grazing on four timber management situations. Southern Journal of Applied Forestry. 7(3): 119-124.

Lundgren, G.K.; Conner, J.R.; Pearson, H.A. 1984. Five forest-grazing management systems in the Southeastern United States. MP-1551. College Station, TX: Texas Agricultural Experimental Station. 8 p.

MacCleery, D.W. 2002. American Forests: A history of resiliency and recovery. Durham, NC: Forest History Society. 58 p.

McKee, W.H., Jr. 1973. Slash pine response to nitrogen and phosphorus on imperfectly drained soil of the West Gulf Coastal Plain. Soil Science Society America Proceedings. 37: 784-788.

McKee, W.H., Jr.; Shoulders, E. 1970. Depth of water table and redox potential of soil affect slash pine growth. Forest Science. 16: 399-401.

McKee, W.H., Jr.; Shoulders, E. 1974. Slash pine biomass response to site preparation and soil properties. Soil Science Society of America Proceedings. 38(1): 144-148.

McLemore, B.F. 1959. Cone maturity affects germination of longleaf pine seed. Journal of Forestry. 57: 648-650.

McLemore, B.F. 1971. Light requirements for germination of loblolly pine seeds. Forest Science. 17(3): 285-286.

McLemore, B.F.; Barnett, J.P. 1966. Storing repellent-coated southern pine seed. Journal of Forestry. 64: 619-621.

McLemore, B.F.; Czabator, F.J. 1961. Length of stratification and germination of loblolly pine. Journal of Forestry. 59: 267-269.

Mann, W.F., Jr. 1971. Early yields of slash pine planted on a cutover site at various spacings. Res. Pap. SO-69. New Orleans: U.S. Department of Agriculture Forest Service, Southern Forest Experiment Station. 16 p.

Mann, W.F., Jr.; Dell, T.R. 1971. Yields of 17-year-old loblolly pine planted on a cutover site at various spacings. Res. Pap. SO-70. New Orleans: U.S. Department of Agriculture Forest Service, Southern Forest Experiment Station. 10 p.

Mann, W.F., Jr.; Derr, H.J. 1970. Response of planted loblolly and slash pine to disking on a poorly drained site. Res. Note SO-110. New Orleans: U.S. Department of Agriculture Forest Service, Southern Forest Experiment Station. 3 p.

Mann, W.F, Jr.; Derr, H.J.; Meanley, B. 1956. A bird repellent for direct seeding of longleaf pine. Journal of Forestry. 54: 190-191.

Mann, W.F., Jr.; Gunter, E.R. 1960. Predicting the fate of fire-damaged pines. Forests & People. 10(1): 26-27, 43.

Mann, W.F., Jr.; Lohrey, R.E. 1974. Precommerical thinning of southern pines. Journal of Forestry. 72: 557-560.

Moehring, D.M. 1964. Speeding up growth of the loblolly. Forest Farmer. 23(6): 9, 13-14.

Moehring, D.M. 1966. Diameter growth and foliar nitrogen in fertilized loblolly pine. Res. Note SO-43. New Orleans: U.S. Department of Agriculture Forest Service, Southern Forest Experiment Station. 3 p.

Morris, L.A.; Jokela, E.J.; O'Conner, J.B., Jr. 1992. Silvicultural guidelines for pinestraw management in the Southeastern United States. Georgia Forest Res. Pap. 88. Atlanta, GA: Georgia Forest Commission, Research Division. 11 p.

Moser, J.C. 1963. Probing the secrets of the town ant. Forests & People. 12(4): 12-13, 40-41.

Nance, W.L.; Shoulders, E.; Dell, T.R. 1985. Predicting survival and yield of unthinned slash and loblolly pine plantations with different levels of fusiform rust. In: Branham, S.J.; Thatcher, R.C., ed. Proceeding of the Integrated pest management research symposium. Gen. Tech. Rep. SO-56. New Orleans: U.S. Department of Agriculture, Southern Forest Experiment Station: 62-72.

Nambiar, E.K.S.; Tiarks, A.; Cossalter, C.; Ranger, J. 2000. Site management and productivity in tropical plantation forests: A progress report. Bogor, Indonesia: Center for International Forestry Research. 112 p.

Newbold, R.A.; Baldwin, C.V., Jr.; Hill, G. 2001. Weight and volume determination for planted loblolly pine in North Louisiana. Res. Pap. SRS-26. New Orleans: U.S. Department of Agriculture Forest Service, Southern Research Station. 19 p.

Nolte, D.L ; Barnett, J.P. 2000. A repellent to reduce mice predation of longleaf pine seed. International Biodeterioration and Biodegradation. 45(3/4): 169-174.

Owston, P.W.; Miller, R.G.; Rietveld, W.J.; McDonald, S.E. 1990a. A quality-control system for improving conifer nursery stock. Tree Planters' Notes. 41(1): 3-7.

Owston, P.W.; Rietveld, W.J.; Barnett, J.P. [and others]. 1990b. A quality control system for improving reforestation success. In: Proceedings, Society of American Foresters National Convention. Washington: Society of American Foresters: 583-584.

Pawuk, W.H.; Barnett, J.P. 1979. Seed handling practices for southern pines grown in containers. Southern Journal of Applied Forestry. 3: 19-22.

Pawuk, W.H.; Barnett, J.P. 1981. Benomyl stimulates ectomycorrhizal development by Pisolithus tinctorius on shortleaf pine grown in containers. Res. Note SO-267. New Orleans: U.S. Department of Agriculture Forest Service, Southern Forest Experiment Station. 3 p.

Pearson, H.A. 1982. Economic analysis of forest grazing. The Stockman. 39(10): 26, 28, 30, 32.

Pearson, H.A.; Baldwin, V.C., Jr.; Barnett, J.P. 1990a. Cattle grazing and pine survival and growth in subterranean clover pasture. Agroforestry systems. 10: 161-168.

Pearson, H.A.; Grelen, H.E.; Epps, E.A. [and others]. 1982. Botanical composition and nutritive value of cattle diets on southern pine range. Res. Pap. SO-178. New Orleans: U.S. Department of Agriculture Forest Service, Southern Forest Experiment Station. 24 p.

Pearson, H.A.; Knowles, R.L.; Middlemiss, P.G. [and others]. 1995. United States agroforestry estate model. Compiler. 13: 27–37.

Pearson, H.A.; Prince, T.E., Jr.; Todd, C.M., Jr. 1990b. Virginia pines and cattle grazing—An agroforestry opportunity. Southern Journal of Applied Forestry. 14: 55-59.

Pearson, H.A.; Rollins, D.A. 1987. Ryegrass pasture for supplementing southern pine native range. Rangelands. 9(1): 19-20.

Pearson, H.A.; Smeins, F.E.; Thill, R.E. 1987. Ecological, physical, and socioeconomic relationships within southern National Forests: Proceedings of the southern evaluation workshop. Gen. Tech. Rep. SO-68. New Orleans: U.S. Department of Agriculture, Forest Service, Southern Forest Experiment Station. 293 p.

Pearson, H.A.; Sternitzke, H.S. 1974. Forest-range inventory: A multiple-use survey. Journal of Range Management. 27(5): 404-407.

Pearson, H.A.; Whitaker. L.B. 1972. Thrice-weekly supplementation adequate for cows on pine-bluestem range. Journal of Range Management. 25(4): 315-316.

Pearson, H.A.; Whitaker, L.B. 1973. Yearlong grazing of slash pine ranges: Effects on herbage and browse. Journal of Range Management. 27(3): 195-197.

Pearson, H.A.; Whitaker, L.B.; Duvall, V.L. 1971. Slash pine regeneration under regulated grazing. Journal of Forestry. 69: 744-746.

Peevy, F.A. 1947. Killing undesirable hardwoods. Southern Lumberman. 175(2201): 123-125.

Peevy, F.A. 1960. Controlling southern weed trees with herbicides. Journal of Forestry. 58(9): 708-710.

Peevy, F.A. 1961. Control of backjack oak by basal spraying with 2,4,5-T. Weeds. 9(1): 50-53.

Peevy, F.A.; Mann, W.F., Jr. 1952. Slash and loblolly pine plantation destroyed by hogs. Forests & People. 2(4): 20, 37.

Powers, R.F.; Alban, D.H ; Ruark, G.A.; Tiarks, A.E. 1990. A soils research approach to evaluating management impacts on long-term productivity. In: Dyck, W.J.; Mees, C.A., eds. Impact of intensive harvesting on forest site productivity. IEA/BE T6/A6 Report No. 2. Rotorua, New Zealand: Ministry of Forestry, Forestry Research Institute: FRI Bulletin No. 159: 127-145.

Powers, R.F.; Tiarks, A.E.; Burger, J.A.; Carter, M.C. 1996. Sustaining the productivity of planted forests. In: Carter, M.C., ed. Growing trees in a greener world: Industrial forestry in the 21st century: 35th LSU forestry symposium. Baton Rouge, LA: Louisiana State University, School of Forestry, Wildlife and Fisheries: 97-134.

Ruehle, J.L.; Marx, D.H ; Barnett, J.P.; Pawuk, W.H. 1981. Survival and growth of container-grown and bare-root shortleaf pine seedlings with Pisolithus and Thelephora ectomycorrhizae. Southern Journal of Applied Forestry. 5: 20-24.

Rumsey, R.L. 1968. A pole's eye view of woodpeckers. Forests & People. 18(2): 20-21, 38-40.

Rumsey, R.L. 1970. Woodpecker attack on utility poles—A review. Forest Products Journal. 29(12): 54-59.

Scott, D.A.; Novosad, J.; Goldsmith, G. 2007. Ten-year results from the North American long-term soil productivity study in the Western Gulf Coastal Plain. In: Furniss, M.; Clifton, C.; Ronnenberg, K. eds., Advancing the fundamental sciences: Proceedings of the Forest Service national sciences conference. Gen. Tech. Report PNW-689. Portland, OR: U.S. Department of Agriculture, Forest Service, Pacific Northwest Research Station: 331-340.

Scott, D.A.; Tiarks, A.E.; Sanchez, F.G. [and others]. 2004. Forest soil productivity on the southern long-term soil productivity sites at age 5. In: Connor, K.F., ed. Proceedings of the 12th biennial southern silvicultural conference. Gen. Tech. Report SRS-71. Asheville, NC: U.S. Department of Agriculture Forest Service, Southern Research Station: 371-377.

Shoulders, E. 1960. Town ants damage slash pine plantations. Southern Forestry Notes 123. New Orleans: U.S. Department of Agriculture Forest Service, Southern Forest Experiment Station: 2.

Shoulders, E. 1976. Site characteristics influence relative performance of loblolly and slash pine. Res. Pap. SO-115. New Orleans: U.S. Department of Agriculture Forest Service, Southern Forest Experiment Station. 16 p.

Shoulders, E. 1983. Comparison of growth and yield of four southern pines on uniform sites in the Gulf Coastal Plain. In: Hotvelt, E.; Jackson, B.D., eds. Predicting growth and yield in the Mid-South. Proceedings 31st annual forestry symposium. Baton Rouge, LA: Louisiana State University: 23-37.

Shoulders, E. 1985. The case for planting longleaf pine. In: Shoulders, E , ed. Proceedings of the 3rd biennial southern silviculture conference. Gen. Tech. Report SO-54. New Orleans: U.S. Department of Agriculture Forest Service, Southern Forest Experiment Station: 255-260.

Shoulders, E.; McKee, W.H., Jr. 1973. Pine nutrition in the West Gulf Coastal Plain: A status report. Gen. Tech. Report SO-2. New Orleans: U.S. Department of Agriculture Forest Service, Southern Forest Experiment Station. 26 p.

Shoulders, E.; Nance, W.L. 1987. Effects of fusiform rust on survival and structure of Mississippi and Louisiana loblolly pine plantations. Res. Pap. SO-232. New Orleans: U.S. Department of Agriculture Forest Service, Southern Forest Experiment Station. 11 p.

Shoulders, E.; Tiarks, A.E. 1980a. Fertilizer fate in a 13-year-old slash pine plantation. Soil Science Society of America Journal. 44(5): 1085-1089.

Shoulders, E.; Tiarks, A.E. 1980b. Predicting height and relative performance of major southern pines from rainfall, slope, and available soil moisture. Forest Science. 26: 437-447.

Shoulders, E.; Walker, F.V. 1979. Soil, slope, and rainfall affect height and yield in 15-year-old southern pine plantations. Res. Pap. SO-153. New Orleans: U.S. Department of Agriculture, Forest Service, Southern Forest Experiment Station. 52 p.

Siggers, P.V. 1932. The brown-spot needle blight of longleaf pine seedlings. Journal of Forestry. 30(5): 579-593.

Snow, G.A.; Rowan, S.J.; Jones, J.P. [and others]. 1979. Using Bayleton® (triadimefon) to control fusiform rust in pine tree nurseries. Res. Note SO-253. New Orleans: U.S. Department of Agriculture Forest Service, Southern Forest Experiment Station. 5 p.

Snyder, E.B.; Derr, H.J. 1972. Breeding longleaf pines for resistance to brown-spot needle blight. Phytopathology. 62: 325-329.

Snyder, E.B.; Dinus, R.J ; Derr, H.J. 1977. Genetics of longleaf pine. Res. Pap. WO-33. Washington: New Orleans: U.S. Department of Agriculture, Forest Service. 24 p.

South, D.B. 2003. "Correct" planting density for loblolly pine depends upon your objectives and who you ask. Forest Landowner Manual. 34: 46-51.

South, D.B.; Barnett, J.P. 1986. Herbicides and planting date affect early performance of container-grown and bare-root loblolly pine seedlings in Alabama. New Forests. 1: 17-27.

South, D.B.; Harris, S.W.; Barnett, J.P. [and others]. 2005. Effect of stock type and stock size on survival and early height growth of Pinus palustris seedlings in Alabama, U.S.A. Forest Ecology and Management. 204: 385-398.

Sternitzke, H.S.; Pearson, H.A. 1974. Forest-range resource statistics for southwest Louisiana Parishes. RB-SO-050. New Orleans: U.S. Department of Agriculture Forest Service, Southern Forest Experiment Station. 22 p.

Sun, X.; Jones, J.P.; Barnett, J.P. 1993. Trichoderma hamatum and T. harzianum vs. Pythium spp. in stored longleaf pine seedling root systems. [Abstract]. Phytopathology. 83: 1352.

Sword, M.A.; Chambers, J.L.; Gravett, D.A. [and others]. 1998. Ecophysiological response of managed loblolly pine to changes in stand environment. In: Mickler, R.A.; Fox, S., eds. The productivity and sustainability of southern forest ecosystems in a changing environment. New York: Springer-Verlag: 185-206.

Sword, M.A.; Tinus, R.W.; Barnett, J.P. 1999. Evaluating the cold hardiness of container longleaf pine seedlings. In: Landis, T.D.; Barnett, J.P., tech. coords. National Proceedings: Forest and Conservation Nursery Association—1998. Gen. Tech. Rep. SRS-25. Asheville, NC: U.S. Department of Agriculture Forest Service, Southern Research Station: 50-52.

Sword Sayer, M.A.; Brissette, J.C.; Barnett, J.P. 2005. New root growth and hydraulic conductivity of southern pine seedlings in response to soil temperature and water availability after planting. New Forests. 30: 253-272.

Sword Sayer, M.A.; Goelz, J.C.G.; Chambers, J.L. [and others]. 2004. Long-term trends in pine productivity and stand characteristics in response to thinning and fertilization in the West Gulf region. Forest Ecology and Management. 192: 71-96.

Sword Sayer, M.A.; Haywood, J.D. 2006. Fine root production and carbohydrate concentrations of mature longleaf pine (Pinus palustris P. Mill.) as affected by season of prescribed fire and drought. Trees. 20: 165-175.

Sword Sayer, M.A.; Haywood, J.D. 2009. Fire and longleaf pine physiology—does timing affect response? In: Proceedings of the 2009 Society of American Foresters convention. Bethesda, MD: Society of American Foresters. 11 p.

Sword-Sayer, M.A.; Tang, Z. 2004. Long-term root growth response to thinning, fertilization, and water deficit in plantation loblolly pine. In: Connor, K.F., ed. Proceeding of the 12th biennial southern silviculture conference. Gen. Tech. Rep. SRS-71. Asheville, NC: U.S. Department of Agriculture Forest Service, Southern Research Station: 458-464.

Tang, Z.; Chambers, J.L.; Guddanti, S ; Barnett, J.P. 1999a. Thinning, fertilization, and crown position interact to control physiological responses of loblolly pine. Tree Physiology. 19: 87-94.

Tang, Z.; Chambers, J.L.; Guddanti, S. [and others]. 1999b. Seasonal shoot and needle growth of loblolly pine responds to thinning, fertilization, and crown position. Forest Ecology and Management. 120: 117-130.

Tang, Z.; Chambers, J.L.; Shufang, Yu; Barnett, James P. 2003. Seasonal photosynthesis and water relations of juvenile loblolly pine relative to stand density and canopy position. Trees. 17: 424-430.

Tang, Z.; Chambers, J.L.; Yu, S. [and others]. 2004a. Reapplication of silvicultural treatments impacts shoot growth and physiology of plantation loblolly pine. In: Connor, K.F., ed. Proceedings of the 12th biennial southern silvicultural research conference. Gen. Tech. Rep. SRS-71. Asheville, NC: U.S. Department of Agriculture Forest Service, Southern Research Station: 450-457.

Tang, Z.; Sword Sayer, M.A.; Chambers, J.L.; Barnett, J.P. 2004b. Interactive effects of fertilization and throughfall exclusion on the physiological responses and whole-tree carbon uptake of mature loblolly pine. Canadian Journal of Botany. 82: 850-861.

Thill, R.E. 1984. Cattle and deer diets on Louisiana pine-bluestem range. Proceedings Southeastern Association Fish and Wildlife Agencies. 36: 410-419.

Thill, R.E. 1986. Deer and cattle diet overlap on Louisiana pine-bluestem range. Journal of Wildlife Management. 50(4): 707-713.

Thill, R.W. 1989. Deer and cattle diets on heavily grazed pine-bluestem range. Journal of Wildlife Management. 53(3): 540-548.

Thill, R.W.; Martin, A., Jr.; Morris, H.F., Jr.; McClure, E.D. 1987. Grazing and burning impacts on deer diets on Louisiana pine-bluestem range. Journal of Wildlife Management. 51(4): 873-880.

Thomas, C.E.; Parresol, B.R.; Kim, H.N. [and others]. 1995. Biomass and taper for trees in thinned and unthinned longleaf pine plantations. Southern Journal of Applied Forestry. 19: 29-35.

Tiarks, A.E.; Haywood, J.D. 1981. Response of newly established slash pine to cultivation and fertilization. Res. Note SO-272. New Orleans: U.S. Department of Agriculture Forest Service, Southern Forest Experiment Station. 4 p.

Tiarks, A.E.; Kimble, M.S.; Elliott-Smith, M.L. 1990. The first location of a national long-term forest soil productivity study: methods of compaction and residue removal. In: Coleman, S.S ; Neary, D.G., comps. Proceedings of the 6th biennial southern silvicultural research conference. Gen. Tech. Rep. SE-70. Asheville, NC: U.S. Department of Agriculture Forest Service, Southeastern Forest Experiment Station: 431-441. Vol. 1.

Tiarks, A.E.; Powers, R.F.; Alban, D.H. [and others]. 1992. USFS long-term soil productivity national research program. In: Kimble, J.M., ed. Utilization of soil survey information for sustainable land use: Proceedings of the 8th international soil management workshop. Lincoln, NE: U.S. Department of Agriculture Soil Conservation Service, National Soil Survey Center: 236-241.

Tinus, R.W.; Sword, M.A.; Barnett, J.P. 1999. Prevention of cold damage to container grown longleaf pine roots. In: Haywood, J.D., ed. Proceedings, 10th Biennial Southern Silvicultural Research Conference. Gen. Tech. Rep. SRS-30. Asheville, NC: U.S. Department of Agriculture Forest Service, Southern Research Station: 331-333.

Wahlenberg, W.G. 1946. Longleaf pine: its use, ecology, regeneration, protection, growth, and management. Washington: Charles Lathrop Pack Forestry Foundation and U.S. Department of Agriculture Forest Service. 429 p.

Wahlenberg, W.G. 1960. Loblolly pine. Its use, ecology, regeneration, protection, growth and management. Durham, NC: Duke University. 603 p.

Wakeley, P.C. 1935. Artificial reforestation in the southern pine region. Tech. Bull. 492. Washington: U.S. Department of Agriculture Forest Service. 115 p.

Wakeley, P.C. 1954. Planting the southern pines. Agric. Monograph 18. Washington: U.S. Department of Agriculture Forest Service. 233 p.

Wakeley, P.C.; Barnett, J.P. 2011. Early forestry research in the South: A personal history. Gen. Tech. Rep. SRS-137. Asheville, NC: U.S. Department of Agriculture, Forest Service, Southern Research Station. 90 p.

Walkinshaw, C.H.; Barnett, J.P. 1995. Tolerance of loblolly pines to fusiform rust. Southern Journal of Applied Forestry. 19: 60-64.

Wolters, G.L. 1982. Longleaf and slash pine decreases herbage production and alters herbage composition. Journal of Range Management. 35(8): 761-763.

Wolters, G.L ; Martin, A.; Pearson, H.A. 1982. Forage response to overstory reduction on loblolly-shortleaf pine-hardwood forest range. Journal of Range Management. 35(4): 443-446.

Wood, J.C.; Blackburn, W.H.; Pearson, H.A.; Hunter, T.K. 1989. Infiltration and runoff water quality responses to silvicultural and grazing treatments on a longleaf pine forest. Journal of Range Management. 42(5): 378-381.

Yeiser, J.L.; Barnett, J.P. 1991. Growth and physiological response of four shortleaf pine families to herbicidal control of herbaceous competition. Southern Journal of Applied Forestry. 15: 199-204.

Yu, S.; Chambers, J.L.; Tang, Z.; Barnett, J.P. 2003. Crown characteristics of juvenile loblolly pine 6 years after application of thinning and fertilization. Forest Ecology and Management. 180: 345-352.

Zarnoch, S.J.; Feduccia, D.P.; Baldwin, V.C., Jr.; Dell, T.R. 1991. Growth and yield predictions for thinned and unthinned slash pine plantations on cutover sites in the West Gulf Region. Res. Pap. SO-264. New Orleans: U.S. Department of Agriculture Forest Service, Southern Forest Experiment Station. 32 p.

Acknowledgments

We thank those who provided constructive comments on early drafts: John Brissette, Anna Burns, Paul Burns, Mason Carter, Helen Derr, Kas Dumroese, Don Feduccia, Bob McLemore, John Moser, and Ron Thill.

We had the privilege of knowing most individuals who worked on the Palustris Experimental Forest and made significant contributions to forestry in the South. We hold them in high esteem and dedicate this publication to them and those technical employees who spent their careers supporting programs conducted on the Experimental Forest.